WRITERS AND THEIR WORK

ISOBEL ARMSTRONG
General Editor

JAMES KELMAN

JAMES KELMAN

Photographed by Jamie Macdonald

JAMES KELMAN

H. Gustav Klaus

NORTHCOTE
BRITISH
COUNCIL

© Copyright 2004 by H. Gustav Klaus

First published in 2004 by Northcote House Publishers Ltd, Horndon, Tavistock, Devon, PL19 9NQ, United Kingdom. Tel: +44 (0) 1822 810066 Fax: +44 (0) 1822 810034.

British Library Cataloguing-in-Publication Data
A catalogue record for this book is available from the British Library

ISBN 0-7463-1064-1 hardcover
ISBN 0-7463-0976-7 paperback

Typeset by PDQ Typesetting, Newcastle-under-Lyme
Printed and bound in the United Kingdom
by Athenaeum Press Ltd., Gateshead, Tyne & Wear

Contents

Acknowledgements

My thanks to Stephen Knight, Livi Michael and John Rignall for reading and commenting on some chapters in this book; to James Kelman for providing biographical information; and to Franziska Wandschneider for tracking and downloading some material from the Internet.

The author and the publishers are also grateful to James Kelman, Polygon, Secker & Warburg and Hamish Hamilton for permission to quote from James Kelman's works.

Biographical Outline

1946	Born 9 June in Glasgow.
1961	Finished school. Apprenticed as a compositor, left the trade two years later.
1963–4	Stayed in Los Angeles and Pasadena, USA.
mid- to late 1960s	Worked in various capacities in Glasgow, Manchester and London, interrupted by spells of unemployment and hitchhiking in Britain and France.
1969	Married Marie Connors. Returned to Scotland.
1972	First story ('He knew him well') published.
1972–5	Attended the Glasgow Writers Group organized by Philip Hobsbaum. Other members included Alasdair Gray, Tom Leonard, Liz Lochhead and Anne Stevenson.
1973	*An Old Pub near the Angel* (short stories) published in Orono, Maine, USA.
1975–8	Studied English and Philosophy at Strathclyde University, Glasgow.
1976	*Three Glasgow Writers* (short stories, with Alex. Hamilton and Tom Leonard).
1978	*Short Tales from the Night Shift*.
1979	Scottish Devolution referendum failed, despite a 'Yes' majority, to reach the stipulated 40 per cent quorum of the electorate. Margaret Thatcher became Prime Minister. Beginning of long Conservative rule.
	Kelman writer-in-residence at Renfrew District Libraries.

1983	*Not Not While the Giro*, the first book-length collection of short stories. Writer-in-residence at Renfrew District Libraries (until 1984).
1984	*The Busconductor Hines* (first novel).
1985	*A Chancer* and *Lean Tales* (with Alasdair Gray and Agnes Owens). *The Busker* staged at the Edinburgh Festival Fringe.
1987	*Greyhound for Breakfast* (short stories) awarded Cheltenham Prize. *In the Night* produced at the Battersea Arts Centre, London.
1989	*A Disaffection* awarded James Tait Black Memorial Prize and shortlisted for the Booker Prize.
1990	Glasgow European City of Culture, boycotted by Kelman and other Glasgow writers. *Hardie and Baird* produced at the Traverse Theatre, Edinburgh. Kelman helps organize the non-academic 'Self-Determination and Power Event' in Glasgow (keynote speaker Noam Chomsky).
1991	*The Burn* (short stories) won a Scottish Arts Council book award. *Hardie and Baird & Other Plays*.
1992	*Some Recent Attacks: Essays Cultural & Political*.
1994	*How Late it Was, How Late* awarded the Booker Prize. *One, Two – Hey!* staged at the Traverse.
1996	Chairman of the People's Tribunal on Racial Violence in Hounslow, London.
1997	Conservatives wiped out in Scotland in general election. Tony Blair became Prime Minister. Referendum on a Scottish Parliament with tax-raising powers carried by a large majority. Kelman one of twenty foreign writers attending a Freedom of Expression Rally in Istanbul.
1998	*The Good Times* (short stories).
1998-9	Taught Creative Writing at University of Texas, Austin.
1999	Elections for Scottish Parliament. Labour and Liberal Democrats form a Coalition Government. Kelman joint holder of the Scottish Writer of the Year award.

2001	*Translated Accounts.*
	Appointed Professor of Creative Writing at University of Glasgow (Chair shared with Alasdair Gray and Tom Leonard).
2002	*'And the Judges Said ... ': Essays.*
2003	Resigned from Chair at Glasgow.
2004	*You Have to be Careful in the Land of the Free.*

References

References are to the first editions listed in the Bibliography.

1

Introduction: 'Fucking Realism'

> James Kelman is a 'Scottish writer', 'a working class writer', 'a political writer', 'a dialect writer', 'a Glasgow writer', 'an angry writer', 'an experimental writer', 'a writer in the tradition of Kafka', 'a writer following Beckett', 'a post-modernist writer'. Any or all these terms might be (and have been) used to identify this most exciting and challenging contemporary author, but they are really no more than flags of convenience.[1]

Ian A. Bell's observation made in 1990 has lost nothing of its pertinence. The proliferation of tags attached to Kelman's work highlights the reputation the author has built among critics, but also the difficulty of coming to terms with an œuvre that now extends to six novels, four major short-story collections, two volumes of cultural and political essays and several plays. It is a body of writing of international renown, as the American editions and the translations into German, French, Spanish, Dutch and Norwegian testify. Although the author was fortunate enough to have his books regularly noticed, and often praised, by the *London Review of Books* and *The Times Literary Supplement* as well as the leading newspapers, he also had, predictably, to contend with another kind of media response. The 1984 chairman of the Booker Prize panel, commenting on the enormity of the task of having to read some eighty novels in as many days, was reported as saying: 'There is even a novel written entirely in what appears to be Glaswegian. Lacking a dictionary I soon gave up!'[2] (The reference was to Kelman's first novel *The Busconductor Hines*.) But this irritation was nothing compared to

1

the chorus of outrage that greeted the decision to award Kelman the prize ten years later for *How Late it Was, How Late*. A dissenting judge called it a 'disgrace'. 'Foul-mouthed novel is a £20,000 Booker winner,' the *Independent* blared. A journalist spoke of 'literary vandalism', and another actually invested time counting how often the word 'fucking' cropped up in the text so as to be able to voice his indignation in a quantifiable way.[3] Booksellers joined in moaning about the failure to sell.[4]

The best thing that can be said about these shrill protests is that they draw attention to the importance of language in Kelman's work. That is what we would expect from any writer. But Kelman has been singular in his determination to think through and carry over into literary practice the implications of the use of voice in narrative texts in English: the voices of the characters in the dialogues, the voices in their heads and the voice of the narrator. The latter worried him especially, for, as he argued in an interview:

> Most people don't think of [it] as 'voice' at all – except maybe the voice of God – and they take for granted that it is unbiased and objective. But it's no such thing. Getting rid of that standard third party narrative voice is getting rid of a whole value system. You have to start examining every term. The example I would use is the term 'beautiful', or 'pretty', or 'handsome', or 'ugly'. There is no possibility of using such a term in my work, not in the standard narrative, it's not a possibility. I can't even say 'fat' or 'thin' because to do that would be to assume a whole value system. None of my work will have any of that whatsoever. This is an extreme example of the kind of formal problems you might have to get through.[5]

As long as narrator and characters move in the same upper circle of society and their language is congruent, this may pose no problem. But once you introduce lower-class characters or write, as Kelman does, about the bottom third of society, a gulf opens in the narrative flow, if the 'third-party' voice adopts standard English as the appropriate accent for authoritative speech and the lower-class characters, when they open their mouths or think, utter 'sub-standard' phrases. In that relation, the vernacular voices, often additionally sealed off from the socially 'superior' accent by 'perverted commas' (Joyce),[6] will inevitably come out as inferior. For Kelman even the best-intentioned working-class writing of the past is marred by this chasm.

In his shorter fiction the author has circumvented the problem by predominantly relying on first-person narrators. I have proposed the term 'speaker-narrator' for these 'I' voices to emphasize the oral demotic quality of their monologic digressions, and to signal the blurring of the borderlines between natural speech and narrative discourse.[7] Several of Kelman's stories would lend themselves to dramatization as radio or stage plays, dramatization not so much in the sense of acted drama – for there is little outward action – but of audible live performance, and one or two have, in fact, been staged or broadcast.

In the first five novels there is no first-person narrator, but it is a measure of the success of Kelman's effort to obliterate, as it were, the narrative voice as an outside interfering agency that in most of them the reader still feels as if there were one. So frequently are we in the minds of the central characters, so compatible are the linguistic registers employed, that it becomes often difficult to decide who is speaking.

Of course, the commentators who waxed indignant over Kelman's language were not concerned with such technical matters at all. The niceties of synonyms for 'pretty' or 'thin' did not interest them a bit. They seized on a detail, which was consequent upon Kelman's rigorously applied method of letting his figures ramble on in their West of Scotland accents and idioms. They picked at the 'disgraceful' language, the 'swear words' in many of his fictions, though by no means all of them (*Translated Accounts*, for example, is a 'fucking'-free novel). The author himself, unsurprisingly, objects to any such labelling on the grounds that it is value-laden, presupposes a hierarchy of discourses and creates ghettos of expression. In Scotland the very term 'bad language' touches on the sensitive issue of a speech-form that has been stigmatized for centuries, not merely 'foul' words but any 'slovenly', 'debased' diction. ' "Everyone should learn to write good English" means "you tinks and keelies, you Paddies, Taffs and Jocks, you Nigs and Pakis, into line there!" '[8]

As against the watchdogs of Pure English and the petty rules of the grammarians, Kelman draws on the unstable forms and anarchic processes of real usage:

Dont tell me yous 're on a bloody go-slow!
A pensioner of the male variety standing on a grass verge by a bus-stop. He seemed to be expecting an answer. This crabbit wee red face shouting on about timetables in a tone of voice that conveyed a total lack of willingness to hear a genuine reply.
But ice-bound roads are always irrelevant in this fucking city. So too the perennial shortage of able bodies. He had stared at Hines with a really fierce expression on the countenance. Abuse was out of the question. What would have been the point, the auld cunt, standing chittering there, a constant drip from the nostrils, in a patch of spare earth, the few thin trees in a kind of formation, waiting for a fucking bus.
Amazing but; how people are conned into thinking high unemployment means parsnips are not in demand. That's the trouble with the lower orders, they're a bunch of bastarn imbeciles.
(*The Busconductor Hines*, p. 122)

It is doubtful whether there is verbal aggression in this passage. The description of the exposure of 'the auld cunt' to the foul weather and bleak townscape is not unsympathetic, though dressed in a rough and superficially unattractive 'speak'. Nor is Hines answering back. But, more important, through sheer repetition and their juxtaposition to 'high'-language words such as 'countenance', 'imbecile' or 'lower orders', expressions like 'fucking', 'cunt' or 'bastarn' are presented as thoroughly normal. One type of word is debunked, the other upgraded in the process: Hines is evidently ridiculing upper-class assumptions about the 'lower orders'.

In fact, the expletives used by Kelman's speakers serve such a wide range of linguistic functions, from fillers and intensifiers to modifiers and exclamations, that no generalized statement about them will do. As insertions in, for example, 'dipfuckingtheria' (*A Chancer*, p. 24) or 'Dysfuckingfunctional Benefit' (*How Late*, p. 248) they show disrespect for high-sounding polysyllables, or articulate ill-feeling against suspicious individuals ('Bufucking-canan' is how Hines thinks of his wife's boss in *The Busconductor Hines*, p. 32). Their object is to help root a character in time, place, situation and mood.

But, it could be argued, to dwell at such length on what is really a side issue is already to concede too much ground to Kelman's detractors. Of greater importance is the author's reliance on the cadences, intonations and syntactical habits of

4

urban Scots; notice, for example, the deferred 'but', a typical feature of Glasgow speech, in the passage quoted above.[9]

None of this makes Kelman 'a dialect writer' if by that is meant a phonetic representation of urban vernacular of the sort we find in the poems of Tom Leonard (for an example, see Chapter 2). 'Glasgow writer' is nearer the mark, except that it risks narrowing down the compass of a work that is of wider relevance than the name of a specific city suggests, for, although it is the scene of most of his narratives, Kelman's fiction is no more simply about Glasgow than Joyce's work is simply about Dublin. If the pubs and betting shops, the grey skies and wet pavements, have a specifically Scottish, or British, flavour, it is nonetheless true that the characters who roam the streets and rubbish dumps, who form the dole queues and survive in the big housing schemes, are beset by problems that can be met in similar locations in Marseilles or Berlin, to say nothing about Moscow or Bucharest since the advent of capitalism.

At every step in Kelman's fiction we encounter problematic characters, neither wholly sympathetic nor totally unlikeable, who are at once stuck in recognizably everyday situations and insoluble existential dilemmas. Inhabitants of the contemporary urban world, they are restlessly yet aimlessly on the move, often feel threatened and sometimes work themselves into a near-paranoid state. The protagonists of the novels, in so far as the term still makes sense for these hamstrung figures, are a bus conductor threatened by unemployment, a compulsive gambler, a sickened teacher at his wit's end, a small crook and an anonymous group of persecutees. The short stories open into a world of snooker halls, racing grounds, park benches, caravan sites and factories. Some of the works take us behind bars. Yet the remarkable thing is that there is nothing unimaginative or brutish about the lives that unfold before us. The picture is not one of grey uniformity or inarticulate monotony, but of endless variation.

'Working-class writer' then? Only if one takes a sufficiently broad view of the concept that does not limit itself to the traditional proletarian novel with which in terms of inventory and narrative technique Kelman has broken; for one looks in vain here for the exceptionally gifted working-class figure, the fighter for the Cause, the working-class hearth and home, the diurnal family life, the archetypal industrial setting, the communal action that were the stock-in-trade of the traditional working-class novel. But it is still true that in reading Kelman one plunges into a universe rarely charted by contemporary English writers, though more frequently so by their Scottish counterparts: the workless and the homeless, the casually and the menially employed, the cadgers and the dodgers, in short the powerless marginalized section of the working class. 'Postmodernist'? Hardly. Kelman has found a way of speaking in his fiction that has nothing to do with the clever mixing and merging of styles and genres (including science fiction, fantasy, gothic or parody) to be found in postmodernism; his high-minded social and philosophical preoccupations cannot be squared with the indeterminate and often ironic stance towards history and politics that we have come to associate with many of its practitioners. If at all, we have to situate him with the Modernists, whose disruption of conventional narrative and defamiliarization of language he shares without merely imitating them.

Rather than continue ticking off the list of tags, it is more sensible to see where Kelman positions himself. There is a short story, 'Naval History', in which a first-person narrator called James bumps into some old friends who tease him about his hobby:

> What d'ye mean what I do for a hobby, what ye talking about now?
> Are ye no still writing your wee stories with a working-class theme?
> My wee stories with a working-class theme . . . Do you mean my plays?
> I thought it was wee stories.
> Well you thought wrong cause it's plays, and it's fucking realism I'm into as well if it makes any difference. (*The Burn*, p. 95)

It certainly makes a difference for the writer James Kelman, whose commitment to this aesthetic practice is absolutely fundamental. 'Realism', he writes in an essay on Alex La Guma (so there can be no mistaking this for a playful fiction), 'is the term used to describe the "the detailing of day-to-day experience" and most writers who advocate social change are realists. . .' Nothing is more crucial nor as potentially subversive as a genuine appreciation of how the lives of ordinary people are lived from moment to moment' (*Judges*, p. 100). This succinct definition gives us materials (glimpses of the lives of ordinary people), an artistic method (a detailed presentation of the concrete and the immediate) and a political position (a commitment to social change), all of which are central to Kelman's vision. It also hints at a relationship between audience, work and writer. 'A genuine appreciation' of everyday lives has both a writer- and reader-oriented dimension, of which the latter aims at the dissemination of realist attitudes.

The realist writing technique, as Kelman understands it, links up with the treatment of voice. 'In a sense, getting rid of the narrative voice is trying to get down to that level of pure objectivity. This is *the* reality here, within this culture. Facticity, or something like that.' Factual reality must be presented as insistently and objectively as possible, so that 'no-one can deny it as *fact*'.[10] Attention to the physical life of the characters, to the minutiae of their little acts, down to such small matters as the rolling of cigarettes or the putting-on of the kettle, has clear priority over artful plotting, which can only distort the untidy reality the characters are faced with. What distinguishes this unrelenting realism from time-honoured naturalism is not only the equally important presentation of the inner life of the characters rendered through extensive interior monologue, but also the refusal to see humans as passive creatures of an overpowering environment. The handling of the characters, the vitality and humour of their voices, keep alive a sense of human potential. The individuals in these fictions doggedly, and sometimes deviously, hold on.

Except in critical orthodoxy, there is no necessary opposition between realism and modernism. All one needs is a sufficiently large and period-independent concept of realism such as that proposed by Brecht in his essay 'Breadth and Variety of the Realist Mode'. Referring to Shelley's 'The Mask of Anarchy', Brecht writes: 'Should this ballad not conform to the standard accounts of the realist mode, then we have to make sure that the accounts of the realist mode are altered, expanded, complemented.'[11] Citing the examples of Cervantes and Swift, he goes on to affirm that realism in no way entails a renunciation of fantasy. In Kelman's realism, that fantasy translates into existential interior monologues expressed in an inventive language that goes beyond a replication of real speech.

Kelman's practice as an 'experimental writer' who is simultaneously a realist puts the lie to the tenacious notion that genuine creativity and technical complexity are incompatible with left-wing political commitment. Just as one can be a distinctly Scottish writer and yet absorb influences from abroad, so one can combine an overt concern for the technicalities of the craft with a strong political challenge. There is no doubt that Kelman's confidence as a writer owes much, and not just in terms of language, to the culture of his native place. From a Scottish viewpoint there is nothing exceptional about the prevalence of working-class life in his fiction. It is one major long-established strand, in the last quarter of the twentieth century perhaps the dominant one. Similarly with the predilection for vernacular voices, even though the rehabilitation of the speech of the city streets is more recent.

Again, to rely on the local has nothing to do with a provincial cast of mind. In Anglo-American discussions of 'provincialism' it has become habitual to quote Patrick Kavanagh's view that a writer's dealings with the parochial, far from being necessarily provincial, can be instances of the universal. Heinrich Böll independently reached a similar conclusion, except that the German language does not distinguish between 'parochial' and 'provincial'. 'It is precisely the Germans' dismissiveness towards the provincial', Böll argues, 'that is provincial. For the provincial is actually the site of the everyday, the social and human. Provinces become places of world literature when language has accrued to them, has been brought to them. Let me only mention Dublin and Prague.'[12]

The debacle of the 1979 referendum was widely felt among the Scots, artists and intellectuals included, who had voted 'Yes' in the hope of obtaining some form of autonomy for their country. Yet the flowering of the arts in Scotland that followed in the 1980s and 1990s, from literature to painting and rock music, was in some ways a direct response to the denial of self-determination in the *polis*, an expression of a 'For a' that' sentiment. Nor was the dissatisfaction targeted exclusively against the Conservative decision-makers in London. When the cream of Glasgow writers boycotted the European City of Culture Year in 1990, which they saw as a publicity event in the service of big business, they turned against a Labour-run Council.

To write from a position on the margins has made many writers sensitive to the reality of colonization, and Kelman is no exception. Like Ngugi wa Thiong'o, he argues the case for *Decolonising the Mind*, when in his Booker Prize acceptance speech he formulates:

> There is a literary tradition to which I hope my work belongs. I see it as part of a much wider process, or movement towards decolonisation and self-determination: it is a tradition that assumes two things, 1) the validity of indigenous culture, and 2) the right to defend it in the face of attack. It is a tradition premised on a rejection of the cultural values of imperial or colonial authority, offering a defence against cultural assimilation. Unfortunately, when people assert their right to cultural or linguistic freedom, they are accused of being ungracious, parochial, insular, xenophobic, racist . . . my culture and my language have the right to exist, and no one has the authority to dismiss that right.[13]

Despite such alertness to the larger issues of colonialism and oppression, Kelman has never lost sight of the smaller struggles nearer home. He has given every kind of practical support to Clydeside Action on Asbestos, to steel workers fighting for the survival of their industry, to initiatives of the unemployed, to saving a Citizens' Advice Office from being scrapped (once again by a Labour Council), to anti-racist campaigns in Glasgow and London. That is to say, Kelman's concern for 'ordinary people' and their problems does not end when he has laid down the tools of the writer. This is in part because he has lived a life close to the people. He has worked on the buses and in factories, though never as a schoolteacher. He has been a gambler and a snooker-player, and as a hitchhiker he has walked the city streets and country roads that feature so prominently in the early short stories.

2

Footloose in Country and City: The Early Short Stories

Although most readers may associate James Kelman with his controversial novels *A Disaffection* (1989) and the Booker Prize-winning *How Late it Was, How Late* (1994), his debut took place in the 1970s, in the short-story genre. These early short stories are not only the author's first accomplished literary productions, they also offer an excellent point of entry into his œuvre. Leaving apart the collection *An Old Pub near the Angel* (1973), which was brought out by a small American publisher and never reached a British audience, his career can be said to have begun with *Three Glasgow Writers* (1976), co-authored with Alex. Hamilton and Tom Leonard. Kelman's portion of this booklet comprises only six stories, yet the selection is a fair indication of things to come. Almost from the start the parameters of Kelman's world are drawn here with a few energetic brush-strokes.

'At least I am elsewhere' (p. 69) is the startling opening of 'Where I Was', a 1,200-word story, in which a nameless solitary vagrant, content to have recently 'absconded' from Glasgow, reflects on his immediate position. He is taking a rest on the roadside after having walked many miles during the day through the Scottish countryside. His low-key satisfaction derives from the safe knowledge that nobody is aware of his present whereabouts, that he is 'well wrapped up' to brave the wintry gale and not short on tobacco, cheese and whiskey. Small things, this survival kit, but from his point of view of immense importance. What may be an uninviting perspective for a cosily installed middle-class reader is thus for the speaker-narrator of this story a cause of minor gratification. Here he is in the middle of nowhere, at 10 o'clock at night, in the downpouring rain, far from any shelter. And 'well wrapped up' turns out to be paper held against his breast by means of a scarf and safety pins. It also means supposedly watertight boots.

The narrator shares his thoughts with us as if this was a perfectly normal state of affairs. He is not out to shock or impress. His set of priorities is simply different. That precisely is Kelman's point. He often confronts us with existences whose everyday life is made up of strategies of survival, who constantly experience defeats but also savour little victories, who doggedly, and sometimes deviously, hold on. As Douglas Gifford has noted, there is a double edge to this kind of portraiture: 'What kind of existence is it that makes its high point out of survival . . . Isn't it amazing how adaptable human beings are that they can cut lower gears which enable them to find sustenance at such low levels of expectation?'[1]

It is not that the 'I' of the story is unconcerned about his health. On the contrary, in what future stories and novels will reveal as a typically Kelmanesque preoccupation, he is quite alert to any possible deterioration of his bodily condition. 'At present I do not even have a running nose. . . . Probably impending bronchitis. . . . Christ I won't be surprised if I catch the flu.' And he spells out in concrete physical detail how 'beads hang onto my eyelashes, cling to my eyebrows, fall from my chin down my neck – from the hair at the back down my neck it streams down my spinal cord' (pp. 70–1). The account becomes increasingly idiosyncratic as he recalls a night in a shut-down youth hostel into which he had forced his way:

> washed both pairs of socks and had a complete body wash which may not have been a good idea since two or three layers of old skin went down the drain. This explains why I am freezing. Unfortunately I am really particular about clean feet and socks. I dont bother about underwear, seldom have any. Up until the wash I was wearing each pair of socks on alternate days, I wore both when sleeping. They had a stale, damp smell. My feet were never wholly dry. Small particles stuck to the toejoints, the soles of the feet. (p. 71)

This brings us to another notable feature of Kelman's developing style. Many of his characters are endowed with a humour that can range from grotesque flights of imagination to subdued self-irony, but serves in most instances, as indeed in the present case, to shield them from the more intolerable aspects of their often hard-pressed existence – and, for the reader, to enliven the text. To welcome 'the exhilarating gale' for 'blowing the dirty scalp clean' (p. 69) is just one example of such self-parody. About the tramp's background or relations we learn nothing, but his voice shows him in command of different linguistic registers. 'Equipage' and 'wayfarers' are as much part of his verbal baggage as 'fucking' and 'bastards'. However, the latter two, sparingly used here, are emphatically not employed as swear words. The remark 'Apparently people do sleep on their feet, the bastards' (p. 71) is in no way a denigration of the homeless. If anything, it expresses sympathy for the footloose who cannot afford a bed at night.

No ordinary vagrant this, then, and there are indeed hints that he may be as much a tramp from choice as from necessity. The thought 'No wonder tramps dont wash' (p. 71) is unlikely to occur to a habitual dosser. However, the point is not to emphasize the singularity of the tramp as tramp, which, instead of cutting through prejudice, would corroborate it, but the individuality of a human being, who happens to have chosen the road, a slightly devious, certainly idiosyncratic, but also self-aware and sophisticated person.

The story does not culminate in any dramatic climax. Nor does it seem to reach any particular point. At the end the narrator's situation has not changed, though he appears rather less cheerful as he slips from the present to the past tense when he reviews his dismal day.

'Where I Was' thus introduces a whole range of features that are characteristic of a good deal of Kelman's short-story writing: the first-person narrator, the solitary being, the itinerant life, the rarely explored milieu of vagrants, the attention to physical detail, the self-irony, the abrupt beginning and the open ending, the sparse outward action. I do not claim that all these features are readily discernible on a first reading. For its momentum and impact to unfold, a Kelman story often requires a second and third reading, and to register its situational and linguistic nuances we need to look at the neighbouring stories in the volume.

'No Longer the Warehouseman' is another fragment of a life's day, again presented as an 'obsessional monologue' (the term is

Alasdair Gray's[2]). The story's opening is similarly arresting: 'What matters is that I can no longer take gainful employment' (p. 62). But already the next two sentences make it clear that the eponymous figure is not a loner, like the tramp, but a family man. The warehouseman has tried, after thirteen months on the dole and the threat now of benefit cuts, to return to the world of paid work, but has failed miserably; he has, in fact, quit his job after only half a day's trial. Despite pangs of guilt, he is also relieved, for inwardly he appears to have renounced his role as a breadwinner ('one feels there is something wrong with one' [p. 62]). He almost searched for a pretext to walk out.

The most interesting aspect of his outpourings is his constant shifting from the 'I' to the distancing 'one'. Whether this is a shamefaced attempt to hush up his personal failure or an indication of a middle-class consciousness, it produces the odd humorous effect, as in the following passage: 'I dislike applying to the social security office. On occasion one has in the past lost one's temper and deposited one's children on the counter and been obliged to shamefacedly return five minutes later in order to uplift them or accompany the officer to the station' (p. 62). The story touches on a social theme – the debilitating effect of unemployment – and, perhaps to emphasize its wider relevance, the locale has been left deliberately vague.

As the warehouseman recounts his altercations with the boss, following his request for his cards, we notice another feature of Kelman's style. Dialogues are not signalled by inverted commas. We notice the absence of quotation marks because we have grown accustomed to this convention, which is still the majority practice in fiction writing. Given Kelman's reliance on first-person narrators who use practically the same kind of demotic speech in their thoughts as in their actual utterances, such a convention becomes quite simply redundant, or worse counterproductive. Inverted commas would re-erect barriers that the author is intent on breaking down. Kelman carries this method sometimes to the point of not even indenting the dialogues. They are completely integrated in the paragraph to keep the narrative flowing: 'I have to leave, I said to him. Well hurry back, replied George. No. I mean I can no longer stay. I am going home . . . What, cried Mister Jackson' (p. 65).

As a narrative (and layout) device, this method obviously takes on greater importance when there is, instead of a first-person narrator, an authorial voice. One of the six stories in *Three Glasgow Writers* is a third-person narrative. The tone of voice of 'Fifty Pence' is detached, impassive, matter-of-fact. 'The old woman opened her eyes when the gas-light flickered, but soon closed them again. With the newspaper raised nearer his eyes the boy squinted at the football news on the back page, trying to find something new to read' (p. 73). In the second paragraph free indirect discourse takes over: 'He glanced at the clock; 8.40. He should have been home by now' (p. 73). At this stage the reader assumes the reference to be to the boy himself. Only in retrospect, when we learn that the woman and the boy, who turns out to be her grandson, are waiting for the grandfather, are we alerted to the possibility that the boy may well have been thinking about him. There is a silent under-standing between the two from which the old man, who eventually returns totally upset, is excluded. They hear him muttering before he is indoors, and he arrives without his usual bonnet. 'Ten shillings I'm telling you' (p. 74). The loss of 50p literally throws him off balance. He sinks on the floor, whether from exhaustion from the fruitless search for the lost coin or because he has been drinking, is unclear but ultimately immaterial. The scene sharply focuses the story once again in poorer Britain, where such a loss is a minor tragedy (as in the previous story there are no place names, this time not even character names). It is also an older Britain, with aged people still thinking in terms of shillings and, strangely, using a gaslight.

The story has something of the atmosphere of the childhood section of *Dubliners*, but freed from any symbolism or epiphany. It is set in the evening, in semi-darkness, in a room where two people are stoically waiting. In Joyce's hands, the boy, who would have been identified, would have experienced some revelation at the sight of his granddad's confusion. Here he simply witnesses the scene, ready to help, only moderately disconcerted, until he is sent home.

In contrast to 'No Longer the Warehouseman' the dialogues in 'Fifty Pence' are laid out in paragraphs:

> He lost money, said the old woman, he said he lost money. That was
> what kept him. He went looking the streets for it and lost his bunnet.
> It's okay, Grannie, the boy said.
> It kept him late, she said. (p. 75)

The text also retains the parentheticals, as linguists call them
('the boy said', 'she said'), which Kelman will often drop in his
later fiction with a view to diminish authorial intrusion. In the
traditional novel the third-person narrative generally went hand
in hand with the use of the past tense. And this is the case here,
too, as opposed to the two 'I' stories considered earlier. But,
while 'Fifty Pence' has a conventional tinge, the gap between
the narrative mode and the speech mode has been narrowed,
for the register of the third-party voice is not above the heads of
the characters. This is in keeping with Kelman's egalitarian
strategy to avoid anything that would present vernacular voices
as inferior.

One more story from *Three Glasgow Writers* deserves a
mention, not only because it enters the rarely explored billiard
world of Glasgow, but because in doing so the narrative stance is
extended from the 'I' to the communal 'we' of public-bar
folklore. 'Remember Young Cecil? He used to be a very Big Stick
indeed' recounts the arrival of a snooker legend on the scene.
Young Cecil quickly becomes the Number 1 stick in the hall and
eventually beats all the players in town. Then a big contest is set
up between him and the Cuddihy brought up from Durham.

> All the daft rumours about it being staged in a football ground were
> going the rounds. . . . Everybody who ever set foot in Porter's was on
> to Cecil that night. And some from down our way who never set foot
> in a snooker hall in their life were on him as well and you cannot
> blame them. The pawn shops ran riot. Everything hockable was
> hocked just to get a bet on Young Cecil. We all went daft. . . . Right
> enough on the day you got the one or two who bet the County
> Durham. Maybe they had seen him play and that, or heard about
> him and the rest of it. But reputations are made to be broke and
> apart from that one or two and Cuddihy and his mates everybody
> else was on Cecil. And they thought they were stonewall certainties!
> How wrong we all were. (pp. 59–60)

Young Cecil meets his fate, and it's his reputation that is broken.
The story lovingly recreates a whole lived subculture, with its
own hierarchies and values.

15

Taking 'Remember Young Cecil?' as an example, Caroline Macafee, in what must be the earliest commentary of Kelman's work, likened the author's mixing of lexical Scots forms with Scottish standard English to John Galt. 'Unlike Galt, however, Kelman also treats the reported speech in the same way, so that the language of the narrator and the characters, who share a social background and milieu, is homogeneous.'[3]

Three Glasgow Writers launched Kelman in Scotland, but it did not launch him alone. He was flanked by the poet Tom Leonard and the fiction and songwriter Alex. Hamilton. Leonard, already a published writer with several slim collections to his credit, is represented with the nine-part sequence 'Unrelated Incidents' and one of his rare excursions into the short story, 'Honest'. Both show him at his unrepenting Glaswegian patter best. Several items from 'Unrelated Incidents' have become well-known anthology pieces, number (7) for example:

> dispite
> thi fact
> thit
> hi bilonged
> tay a
> class uv
> people
> thit hid
> hid thir
> langwij
> sneered
> it
> since hi
> wuz born . . .

(p. 41)

What clearly unites Leonard with Kelman is the concern for the unprinted voice, the language as it is really used in the streets, which in the 1970s was still widely regarded, even in his native Scotland, as 'thi lang-/ wij a thi / guhtr' (thus item 1 of the sequence) and in any case considered unfit for literary use. Kelman, who became a close friend of Leonard's, was so impressed by the latter's successful phonetic representation of speech sounds and the actual dynamics of expression, with its attention to a speaker's hesitations, halts and repetitions, that he did not continue writing in Glaswegian *patois* after 'Nice to be Nice' (in *An Old Pub near the Angel*) and 'The Hon' (discussed below).[4]

There are other parallels. Just as Kelman is not bent on symbols, so Leonard has no patience with conceited metaphors. He may, however, play on words, as with the title 'Unrelated Incidents', which suggests not only that the issues raised in the sequence are, at first sight, unconnected, disparate, but also that they have been untold, suppressed. Both Leonard and Kelman are uncompromising champions of the underclass, sensitive to all aspects of social injustice, including people's denial of the worth of their own language.

It is equally instructive to read Alex. Hamilton's stories alongside Kelman's, if for different reasons. Initially they seem indistinguishable from one another: 'What I mean is, I know Andy's my mate and maybe you shouldn't criticise your pals too much, because then the folk that aren't his mates can sometimes take advantage of what you say and so it gets back to him – and then where are you? Sometimes he goes too far though: I'll just put it that way' (p. 15). This could be a Kelman opening: a rambling 'I' voice taking us into confidence. But we soon notice that Hamilton's figures do not so much draw us into their minds as engage in action. And with the first dialogue come the inverted commas and a phonetic description of Glasgow Scots that Kelman is so anxious to avoid since they spell for him the pitfalls of patronization. In an interview a decade later, he spoke of a 'wee game going on between writer and reader': 'They speak in the same voice as the narrative, and they're unlike these fucking natives who do the dialogue in phonetics . . . In other words, the person who speaks is not as good, or rather not as intellectually aware as the writer or reader.'[5] To be sure, this swipe was not aimed at his co-author. He targeted other, especially middle-class writers. But the issue helps to clarify where Kelman and Hamilton (and a host of well-intentioned working-class writers) part company. They start out on the same terrain – that is, an attempt to get into writing the experiences of a social group that has either been submerged in literary history or misrepresented in clichéd terms. This group includes the tramps, unemployed or casual workers, old-age pensioners, billiard players and pub-goers we encountered in Kelman's stories, and the working-class youths from the housing schemes in Hamilton's.[6]

Three Glasgow Writers, then, was a concerted, if limited attempt to put Glasgow on the literary map in a manner that transcended the vision of the social-realism school of the past, which had concentrated on the gloomy, degrading, nauseating side of the city. That is why the clichéd slum, gangland and soccer (violence) images of Glasgow are absent from these pages, and why a sense of human potential is kept alive amid stifling social realities. As Leonard's speaker in the above-quoted 'dispite / thi fact' poem continues:

> dispite
> a long
> history uv
> poverty n
> thi
> violence uv
> people in
> positions
> uv
> power telln
> him his
> culture wuz
> a sign
> of his
> inferiority
> (. . .)
> this
> ordinary wurkn
> man got
> up wan day
> n
> wuz herd
> tay rimark
> thit
>
> it wuzny
> sitcha
> bad day
> tay be
> alive

(pp. 41–2)

18

In the autobiographical note to his selection Kelman himself
waxed poetical on this loyalty to place:

> I was born and bred in Glasgow
> I have lived most of my life in Glasgow
> It is the place I know best
> My language is English
> I write
> In my writings the accent is in Glasgow
> I am always from Glasgow and I speak English always
> Always with this Glasgow accent
>
> This is right enough

(p. 51)

It is a loyalty the author has kept – the blurb to his 1992
collection of essays *Some Recent Attacks* states wryly that 'James
Kelman lives and will probably die in Glasgow' – but this should
not be confounded with local chauvinism. All he says here is
that the 'accent', the idioms and cadences of the voices, are 'in
Glasgow'. However, in the short stories Kelman's Glasgow is
seldom a clearly identifiable place. It is not often that one can
follow a character's movements with the finger on the map, as
one can, say, James Joyce's *Dubliners*. In a talk to students on
'The Importance of Glasgow in my Work', he put it that way:
'The stories I wanted to write would derive from my own
background, my own socio-cultural experience. I wanted to
write as one of my people, I wanted to write and remain a
member of my own community' (*Attacks*, p. 81). Not to write
himself out of his community as had happened to so many
writers, including Joyce or D. H. Lawrence, was one thing, but 'it
should be kept in mind that Glasgow can be any other town or
city in Great Britain, including London, Edinburgh, Cardiff,
Cambridge, Newcastle or Ramsgate' (*Attacks*, p. 80).

The six stories in *Three Glasgow Writers* amounted to no more
than 9,000 words. The ten *Short Tales from the Night Shift*,
published in 1978, was an even slimmer effort, the print run of
500 copies yet smaller. But the new collection was a single-
handed publication and showed Kelman as master of the
miniature form, the very short short story. Not one piece goes
over more than a page, several consist of a single paragraph, and
the shortest and most famous does not exceed a dozen lines:

In this factory in the north of England acid was essential. It was contained in large vats. Gangways were laid above them. Before these gangways were made completely safe a young man fell into a vat feet first. His screams of agony were heard all over the department. Except for one old fellow the large body of men was so horrified that for a time not one of them could move. In an instant this old fellow who was also the young man's father had clambered up and along the gangway carrying a big pole. Sorry Hughie, he said. And then ducked the young man below the surface. Obviously the old fellow had had to do this because only the head and shoulders . . . in fact, that which had been seen above the acid was all that remained of the young man.[7]

There is fierce, if oblique social comment in this breath-taking story – only strengthened by the unemotional stance of the narrator – and yet there is also something else, a sense of the macabre, with which the narrator through his intrusion ('Obviously the old fellow had had to do that') seems to collude. When Alasdair Gray published his celebrated novel *Lanark* in 1981 he embedded the story in his catalogue of 'diffuse plagiarisms' and thus secured it a wider audience than the *Night Shift* collection alone could ever have hoped for.[8]

There are fewer factory sketches here than the title would lead one to expect. Only one other item matches 'Acid' in this respect, the no less gruesome 'The Habits of Rats' about the almost lethal blood poisoning of a storeman who had his sandwiches urinated upon by the rodents. In two others factory work looms in the distance. One of these, 'The Hon', is written entirely in urban Scots. This is the opening:

Auld Shug gits oot iv bed. Turns aff the alarm cloak. Gis straight ben the toilit. Sits doon in that oan the lavatri pan. Wee bit iv time gis by. Shug sittin there, yoning. This Hon. Up it comes oot fri the waste pipe. Stretchis right up. Grabs him by the bolls. Jesus Christ shouts the Shug filla.

The Hon gis slack in a coupla minits. Up jumps Shug. Straight ben the kitchin hodin onti the pyjama troosirs in that jist aboot collapsin inti his cher.

Shug will miss more than his shift. When his wife comes in she sees that he is dead and faints beside him. 'Lyin ther. The two iv them. Wan in the cher in wan in the fler.' In comes the grown-up daughter. 'Merrit hersel. Mans a bad yin bit [*sic*]. Cunts nevir worked a day in his life. Six weans tay.'[9]

In economy and precision these terse clipped sentences in the present tense are not second to the minimalism of 'Acid'. Between them, 'Acid', 'The Habits of Rats' and 'The Hon' take us into an as yet unknown region of Kelman's universe. Read in the order presented here – in the original volume 'The Hon' preceded the other two – they reveal a growing sense of the terrifying intruding into the everyday texture of our lives. 'Sarah Crosbie', the remaining third-person tale in the collection, also belongs here, with its paraphernalia of uncanny elements (a dead man's body, a haunted house, a deranged woman). The intriguing thing about Kelman's method is that the narrative rests at once in a firmly realist mode and is undercut by a black deadpan humour. It is tempting to relate this fusion to the archetypal Scottish twinning of opposites where the ordinary meets the fantastic. Such a view runs counter to Kelman's propagated self-image as a writer more steeped in a European than a native tradition.

However this may be, Kelman did not pursue this line of stories. He may have felt that they depend too much on dramatic incident. Another reason may be their location in the traditional centres of working-class life, the factory and the home, whereas around him settled industrial communities crumpled one after another under the onslaught of enforced deindustrialization and the movement of capital into more profitable places. It is the consequent displacement and fragmentariness of existences no longer bound by a close-knit community that are explored in several 'I' narratives in the *Night Shift* collection. If they have nothing to do with factory work, they may yet be yarns spun or thought over during a night shift.

'Manufactured in Paris' is close in tone and situation to 'Where I Was'. The city tramp searching a dump for a pair of decent boots is as concerned about the state of his feet as his country cousin. And he can be as sarcastically humorous: 'Cant make you a pair of shoes these days. More comfort walking about in a pair of mailbags.' So he keeps hankering after a French pair that lasted him for months. The narrator of 'Busted Scotch' is looking forward to a Friday gambling night with 'the first wage from the first job in England'. He bets his entire earnings and promptly loses. Told in a more contorted manner, this is also an experience made by the educated narrator of 'An

21

Enquiry Concerning Human Understanding' who has backed a horse that, leading by several lengths, falls at the last hurdle. As the win slips through his fingers, his cultivated voice slips into a lower register: 'Ach, Fuck that for a Game.' Down-at-heel thus meets down-on-their lucks in these pages, solitary itinerant lives hinging on chance, with no stability or security in sight.

The haunting quality of some of Kelman's short stories observed above returns in different guise in 'The Witness'. This has a dark menacing aspect, unrelieved by any flights of humour. A first-person narrator observes a sleeper awakening and dressing to get out of the room. Hardly a word passes between them. The next thing he witnesses through a gap in the doorway is a struggle between the man and a female. 'He began to strike her about the shoulders, beating her down onto her knees; and she cried, cried softly.' The reader is disturbed not only by the sudden outbreak of violence – rarely met in Kelman's early fiction – but also by the narrator's gazing passivity: 'This was the *thing*. I held my head in both hands.' So much remains enigmatic in this tale. What is the relationship between the three unnamed characters? Why does the woman not shout for help, but 'cried softly'? What does the narrator mean by the *'thing'*?

An interim stocktaking is now possible. What we get in these stories are glimpses of existences rather than extensive lifelines. Between these individual figures there is endless variety, often to the point of idiosyncrasy. These particular traits emerge through their thought processes and interaction with others, never through authorial guidance. We do not learn what they look like, only what it looks like inside them. Many, though by no means all of them (a frequent but incorrect generalization of the author's work) lead itinerant, haphazard, isolated lives. And, finally, this is very much a male preserve. Women are conspicuous by their absence or subservience.

On the strength of these pamphlet-size collections no major publisher in Scotland, let alone London, seemed as yet prepared to stake its money on a Kelman book. It was not until 1983 that Polygon, the student-run imprint of Edinburgh University Press, signed a contract for a book-length collection of stories. Polygon was then directed by Peter Kravitz, in whose hands it became a springboard for many budding Scottish writers. Agnes Owens

(1984), Ian Rankin (1986), Janice Galloway (1989), A. L. Kennedy (1990), to name but a few, all had their first novel published by Polygon before metropolitan presses took them over. The strangely titled *Not Not While the Giro* was an instant success. Isobel Murray in the *Scotsman* found it a 'very disturbing book. And a very distinguished one.' Carl MacDougall in the *Times Educational Supplement* saw 'the achievement of a unique voice'. In *British Book News* Donald Campbell celebrated the advent of a 'highly individual and intensely interesting practitioner of the art of the short story', while Elaine Jordan in the *London Review of Books* lauded the vitality of the writing 'which can only come from economy and a grim Glaswegian humour that surmounts helplessness and dereliction'.[10] These were in the main Scottish critics, but their reviews reached an all-British audience. No wonder that the collection also did commercially well – a reprint was due in 1985 – so that two further contracts from Polygon for the novels *The Busconductor Hines* and *A Chancer* followed.

Not Not While the Giro collects some of the work of the 1970s – three stories from the American volume *An Old Pub near the Angel*, another three from *Three Glasgow Writers* and two from *Short Tales from the Night Shift* – but adds twice as many new pieces written or completed since 1978. The book begins with an account of a suicide and ends with the contemplation of one. But, despite material deprivation lurking everywhere, despair or depression is not the keynote, rather a nervous restlessness of people shifting and drifting about, the vast majority of them single units, male and mostly under 40, unbound by family ties or friendships. 'My planning never seems to allow of action of an intentional nature' (*Giro*, p. 145), confesses the narrator of 'Keep moving and no questions', and this aimlessness and indecision are widespread. There is an overwhelming inability or unwillingness to stay in a fixed abode or occupation. Those who are not downright unemployed (like the characters in 'An old pub near the Angel', 'Ten guitars', 'Nice to be nice', 'Charlie', 'Remember Young Cecil' [the title has been abridged], 'Not not while the giro') are either in casual jobs such as building and tank cleaning ('The bevel', 'The hitchhiker') and potato-picking ('Zuzzed'), threatened by redundancy ('Double or clear plus a tenner') or quitting on their own account ('No longer the warehouseman' [title now in lower case], 'The block', 'A wide runner'). Economic pressure is omnipresent. We are more often below than above the poverty line. The hope of these haphazard existences for a scrap of good fortune is epitomized by their penchant for punting or gambling ('Nice to be nice', 'Remember Young Cecil', 'A wide runner', 'Double or clear plus a tenner').

The restlessness with which these characters are beset is also reflected in their temporary accommodation: caravans ('The bevel', 'The hitchhiker'), digs ('Charlie'), a tent ('Zuzzed'), a bedsit evicted from ('Ten guitars') or left without payment ('An old pub near the Angel'), rooms in houses rented on a weekly basis ('Charlie', 'The house of an old woman'). Some sleep rough ('A wide runner', 'Keep moving and no questions'). An owned dwelling is as remote a possibility as a secure position.

Relations between the sexes, where they occur, are equally transitory, little more than fugitive encounters ('Ten guitars', 'Keep moving and no questions', 'The hitchhiker'). Although we hear of family men ('Nice to be nice', 'Jim dandy', 'No longer the warehouseman', 'Wee horrors', '*le joueur* ' [I take the title '*le jouer*' to be a misprint]) their wives remain offstage. Compare this with the obsession with gender relations, and especially sex, in the general run of contemporary *English* short fiction as exemplified by Martin Amis, Malcolm Bradbury, David Lodge, Adam Mars-Jones, Fay Weldon and others in *The Penguin Book of Modern British Short Stories*, and a world of difference opens with regard not only to the social milieu but also to the preoccupations.

If we break down the volume into recognizable locations, Glasgow appears hardly more often than London (eight times as against six), thus bearing out Kelman's observation that 'Glasgow can be any other town or city in Great Britain'. The consistency is one of urban landscape rather than specific place. The impression of some readers that this is all a Clydeside universe may derive from the idioms and accents of the speaker-narrators in a volume where 'I' narratives vastly outnumber omniscient perspectives.

Words like 'wee' and 'broo' (for the Labour Exchange), the adjective 'bastarn' and 'weans' give away the Scottish identity of the protagonists. All these expressions turn up in the long title story, which takes the form of an extended interior monologue, broken up in neatly spaced-out shorter and longer paragraphs.

Some of these resemble diary entries, in others the speaker-narrator calls himself to order. 'Utter rubbish. How in the name of christ can one possibly consider suicide when one's giro arrives in two days' time' (p. 192). Equally alternating are the narrator's moods, swinging from anguished self-doubt and near-desperation, tempered only by self-irony, to delirious fantasizing. Here is his sardonic self-assessment as an employable person: 'If I were an Industrial Magnate or Captain of Industry I would certainly entertain doubts as to my capacity for toil. I am an idlegoodfornothing. A neerdowell. The workhouse is too good for the likes of me. I own up. I am incompatible with this Great British Society. My production rate is less than atrocious' (p. 196). Confined to his quarters, this is the most solipsistic and self-absorbed character in the book and simultaneously the most richly articulate. His dole-caused inertia contrasts starkly with his grotesque flights of imagination. All he does is smoke (the last two cigarettes, keenly registered), drink tea, sign on at the 'broo', have a pee, listen to the noises in the house – and wait and think. The more unbearable this futile expectancy becomes, the more he immerses himself in fantasies of escape. In a grand finale he pictures himself walking from Land's End to John O'Groats and back for the rest of his life:

> And with pendants and flags attached to the suitcase I could beg my grub & tobacco. The minimum money required. Neither broo nor social security. The self sufficiency of the sweetly self employed. I could be for the rest of my life. The Land's End to John O'Groats man. That would be my title. My name a byword . . . if it takes 6 weeks a trip and the same back up I could average 4 return trips a year. If I am half way through life just now ie. a hundred and twenty return trips then in another hundred and twenty trips I would be dead. I can mark off each trip on milestones north & south. And when the media get a grip of me I can simply say I'll be calling a halt in 80 trips time.   (p. 205)

Or if this ersatz activity is over the top he could still pose as the Scottish Coastroad Walker:

> While the hot days in central summer are the busloads of tourists arriving to see me, pointed out by their driver, the Legend of the North, the solitary trudging humpbacked figure with dog & gnarled staff just vanishing out of sight into the mist. Dont give him money Your Lordship you'll just hurt his feelings. Just a bit of your cheese piece and a saucer of milk for the whelp.   (p. 206)

The quotation conveys something of the flavour of Kelman's restless monologues, the wit and idiosyncrasy of the speaker-narrators. It is through the language, through their thought, not through any conspicuous acts of defiance, that so many of these hard-pressed characters display their resilience in the face of overwhelming odds.

The *Giro* volume is also interesting for the rare insight it affords into the evolution of Kelman's style. Three of the first four stories come from *An Old Pub near the Angel*, and, while the pubs, dole queues, bedsits or single-ends in which we meet the characters of these stories are familiar territory, some of them display technical features that will disappear in the subsequent writings. The opening sentences of the first two stories are nothing if not conventional. 'The old man lowered the glass from his lips and began rolling another cigarette.' ('He knew him well', p. 9). Typically Kelmanesque activities these may be, but as an opening it is as pedestrian as 'Charles wakened at 9.30 and wasted no time in dressing' ('An old pub near the Angel', p. 13). What a difference to the striking beginnings of 'No longer the warehouseman', quoted above and reprinted here, or of the title story, which starts in mid-sentence: 'of tea so I can really enjoy this 2nd last smoke which will be very very strong which is of course why I drink tea with it in a sense to counteract the harm it must do to my inners' ('Not not while the giro', p. 182). This throws us right into the skull of the narrator. The first three stories in the volume are also uncustomary in retaining the speech marks that the author abandoned in the later 1970s collections. Finally, 'An old pub near the Angel' has an awkwardly obtrusive because abrupt transition from third-person to first-person narrative (as interior monologue), and consequent substitution of present tense for past.

I have not listed these points in order to show up inconsistencies in Kelman's handling of the genre, merely for the historical record. 'He knew him well' was the author's first published short story,[11] and the other two followed closely on its heels. That Kelman in subsequent collections never included the other ten stories from *An Old Pub near the Angel* shows the distance he had travelled from his earliest endeavours.[12]

The reception of *Not Not While the Giro* made Kelman a writer to be reckoned with, and reviewers were looking forward to his announced first novel. But it would take another two years for a first metropolitan publication to materialize. The occasion was *Lean Tales* (1985), which once again brought together a trio of writers. In his postscript to the volume, Alasdair Gray, one of the three, recounts the genesis of the book. He had followed his widely acclaimed first novel *Lanark* (1981) with a collection of *Unlikely Stories, Mostly* (1982), the paperback rights of which had been bought by Penguin.

> A director of a London publishing house asked him if he had enough stories to make another collection. Gray said no. There was a handful of stories he had intended to build into another collection, but found he could not, as he had no more ideas for prose fictions. From now on he would write only frivolous things like plays or poems, and ponderous things like A History of the Preface.[13]

That is how Kelman and Agnes Owens came in. The latter had been discovered by the other two when they were tutoring part-time for Glasgow University's Adult Education Department.

Kelman and Gray (as well as, among others, Tom Leonard) in turn had benefited from belonging to the Glasgow Group of Writers run by Philip Hobsbaum, outside the university. Hobsbaum's magnetic influence on writers, wherever he taught (previously London and Belfast), deserves a footnote in the post-war history of British culture.[14] After the group had disbanded in 1975, several of its members clubbed together to form the writers' cooperative Print Studio, where they published each other's work in smallish volumes, among them Liz Lochhead's *Islands* (1978), Tom Leonard's *If Only Bunty Was Here* (1979), Alasdair Gray's *The Comedy of the White Dog* (1979) and Kelman's *Short Tales from the Night Shift*. How important this fellowship of local writers was, and is, for Kelman is revealed in the dedication of *How Late it Was, How Late* (1994):

> Alasdair Gray, Tom Leonard, Agnes Owens
> and Jeff Torrington
> are still around,
> thank christ

The last-named might, like Owens, never have made it into print if Kelman had not sponsored and worked with him on his novel *Swing hammer swing!* (1992), brought out by what had meanwhile become Kelman's publisher, Secker & Warburg, where fellow-Scot Robin Robertson proved a congenial editor. All these writers are to a large extent self-taught. Several came late to publishing. Gray was 47, Torrington 57, Owens 59, when their first books were published. Between them, they have helped establish Glasgow's reputation as a fertile literary place. Kelman's section in *Lean Tales* does not extend the now familiar range of personnel, interests and preoccupations – in fact, a good deal of the material stems from *Three Glasgow Writers* ('Where I Was', 'The City Slicker and the Barmaid') and *Short Tales from the Night Shift* (six items) – but the stories assembled here accentuate certain tendencies that are now unrelieved by other effects such as the communal spirit of 'Remember Young Cecil', the humorous side of 'Not not while the giro' or the childhood nostalgia of 'Fifty Pence' and 'Away in Airdrie'. The outlook in *Lean Tales* is altogether bleaker. Only four characters in these eighteen stories work, and of these only one appears to have a regular position. Menial temporary jobs are the rule, so that it comes as no surprise to find a sweeper-up chucking it all in – the by-now familiar story – after half a day ('Extra Cup'). The one gainfully employed person is tellingly a nightboiler-man, who works in complete isolation and appears to be happiest when he is in the basement, at the greatest possible distance from any living soul. Shut away from the world, he occasionally comes up for a smoke with the 'Nightoutsideman'. Whatever communion there is between the two takes place in silence: 'We exchange nods. . . . He raises his eyebrows, a brief smile. He smiles a lot, speaks very rarely; he just likes to sit there, watching the things that happen . . . . Now and then he will gesture at the sky' ('A Nightboilerman's Notes', *Lean Tales*, pp. 91–2).

Lean Tales is especially densely populated by footloose men. Married exemplars have disappeared altogether. It is everyone for himself (this is still an exclusively male world). Social relations have dwindled further. Considerations of a family member, girlfriend or even mate do not enter the rambling minds of these loners – there are only 'I' narratives left now – even though one or two may still fantasize about women ('the paperbag', 'The City Slicker and the Barmaid'). Chance meetings are as inconsequential as before.

This is ever more life on the margins, but the point is that the margin has widened and enclosed more people, as the pinch of Thatcherite policies came to be felt. In the first half of the 1980s the social situation had deteriorated dramatically on the Clyde and in other depressed areas. In and around Glasgow one in four of the workforce was unemployed, with the result that poverty had risen 'by 46 per cent from 1981–86. More than a quarter of the local population, 28 per cent, now live at or below the poverty line: this figure includes almost a third of the region's children, 42 per cent of its old people, 67 per cent of its registered unemployed and 67 per cent of its single parents'.[15]

Kelman's protagonists belong with the losers in Mrs Thatcher's grandiose design of a modernized Britain. And it is not material loss alone with which they have to cope. The demoralization of the speaker-narrator in 'the same is here again', reduced to a life in the streets, his body ravaged, his mental breakdown imminent, is real enough. But, to go to the other end of the spectrum, the case of the happily employed nightboilerman demonstrates that there is a more general malaise afflicting these characters: a deep loneliness, an inability to connect, an anguish, a purposelessness and indecision, a sense of confinement, in short a state of alienation. There is no way out of this crisis, no escape route open. Social mobility, in any case, is only downward. In inhabiting the same cordoned-off territory, these misfits are exposed to the same invisible, yet inexorable structures determining their life. All they can do, each in his own way, is face up to this essential condition, hold on, get by, refuse to be cowed, resist cracking. This they achieve with mixed results, by sometimes astonishingly resourceful means, including devious ones. We are treading on existentialist ground here, something that will require further discussion when we look at the novels.

3

Unsettlingly Settled: *The Bus-conductor Hines* and *A Chancer*

After all the solitary and rootless lives in the short stories, the family and workplace setting of *The Busconductor Hines* (1984) appears to signal a change in Kelman's fictional direction:

> Hines jumped up from the armchair, she was about to lift the huge soup-pot of boiling water. She nodded when he said, I'll get it. Taking the dishtowel from her he wrapped it round his left hand before gripping the metal support-ring; he held the handle of the pot in his right hand. He raised it slightly above the oven and paused, adjusting to its weight. Sandra had moved to shift a wooden chair out of his path.
>
> The plastic babybath was positioned a yard from the fire with several sheets of newspaper spread beneath and around it. She had already emptied in a basinful of cold water. After each step across he was pausing to let the water settle. When he reached it he tilted the soup-pot a little at a time, until about a quarter of the water remained, then he emptied that straight in. What a weight, he said.
>
> I put in too much . . . She had returned to the oven for a smaller pot of water which was also boiling . . .
>
> Before putting the empty pots back into their place in the kitchen-cabinet she wiped them dry with the dishtowel. Then she undressed. She stopped, and walked to draw the venetian blind at the window above the sink. Hines smiled. Passing helicopters eh!   (p. 9)

The opening of *The Busconductor Hines* achieves many things at once. It shows Rab Hines as an attentive, caring, tender fellow; a moment later he will offer to massage and wash Sandra's back. It places the couple socially, in a flat without bathroom and hot water, compelled to use old-fashioned methods for a proper wash (we are, after all, in the 1970s). The 'babybath' suggests a child in the house, though the little boy, no longer a baby, is not introduced until several pages later. The real shock is the spectacle of an adult using the small plastic tub, and the realization that, in order to enjoy the comfort of a hot bath that everyone nowadays just takes for granted, Sandra (and countless others in the same milieu) runs the risk of scalding herself. It is a domestic 'Acid' situation, less horrendous only because it does not end in disaster. Finally, Hines's joke about the 'passing helicopters' reveals his sense of humour, and on the next page, still in the same scene, he is shown to be a book-reader.

What the quoted passage does not show but subtly hints at, as the scene is developed, is some kind of reticence on Sandra's part. When Hines, slightly amused, watches her crouched in the tub with her bra still on, he is sexually stirred, and his massage is part-erotic, but in not responding she stops him.

We get a set of impressions the significance of which we cannot yet fathom. But as the story unfolds it becomes clear that they are not random elements. Hines's devotion as a family man, his attachment to his wife, Sandra's dissatisfaction with the poorly equipped flat, the growing estrangement between the two – these are central elements of the story. But the author makes no concession to the lazy reader. One has to read on and reread previous passages in order to form a fuller picture of the situation. Thus it is not until we are two-thirds through the novel that we get a closer description of the century-old crumbling tenement and its equally deteriorating neighbourhood, or that we learn something about Hines's past, on first meeting Sandra in a bus.

One reason for this delay is that from the start we follow the action through Hines's eyes. In fact, we enter his mind in the very first sentence. And it is the comma between the two clauses of that sentence that makes this clear. A semi-colon would have implied a neutral vantage-point from which the movements of the two figures are studied, whereas 'she was about to lift the huge soup-pot of boiling water' is Hines's observation of his wife's preparations for the bath. In an interview Kelman has also argued that a comma is less intrusive. A semi-colon in an opening sentence 'puts too much emphasis onto it . . . makes it emphatic, you know. It's got to be something that's so everyday.'[1]

The family is one pole of Hines's existence, the buses the other. This dual aspect is underlined by the collocation in the novel's title (job designation plus family name). In the second scene we find him in the company of other conductors and drivers. It is an almost caricatural masculine world complete with booze, loud-mouthed talk and violence. The macho conventions to which Hines tunes in here stand in sharp contrast to his behaviour at home. And the juxtaposition of these two scenes at once acknowledges the persistence of male working-class rituals and highlights how far Hines, as conscientious househusband and loving father, has moved away from this tough, drink-crazed and aggressive type. Overcome by self-pity at one point he will affirm 'that men have every right to greet' (p. 163), and when, accompanied by his son, he challenges the garage bosses, he becomes so emotional that even in public he can hardly hold back his tears.

So the 'macho' incident is relativized, and it would be equally wrong to mistake the expletives 'fucking' and 'cunt', which the workmates hurl at each other, for hateful venom. The banter and repartee between Hines and his regular driver Reilly, for instance, are more remarkable for their good-natured and verbally dextrous altercations than for semantic aggression. Reilly has called Hines an 'orange bastard' only to be told off as a 'typical fenian marxist fucking glory seeker'. Again, this exchange acknowledges the continuity of the religious and ethnic divisions of Clydeside while not exploiting them in sensationalist ways (as some Glasgow novels in the past have done):

> [Reilly] According to what I heard you were jacking the job.
> Hines shook his head. I'v never met a cunt like you for the poking the nose in where it doesnt belong. I'm no kidding you Reilly you're a disgrace to the Vatican.
> Here we go, evasion of the issue; typical Masonic trick.
> I'd rather be a Mason than a Pope.   (p. 33)

Hines waxes indignant over Reilly's candidature in the forthcoming shop-steward elections:

> An Inspectorship; that's what you're really after. Everything's fitting the gether by christ. Once I jack the job you'll be applying for the one-man fucking bus training then after that you'll be grabbing the Shop Stewardship while sneakily entering the Inspector's exam. O

for fuck sake and then it'll be the Deskclerkship! Too much! You and Campbell. The plot's out. Imagine it too; the cunt's too embarrassed to confide in me. Me! His one genuine mucker in the entire garage spectrum. (p. 34)

It is true that Hines is suspicious of every kind of authority, from Transport Service Inspectors, in whose books he figures all too often, right up to the 'entrempeneurial mejisteh' (p. 91), of whom he warns his son. And he smells careerism in Reilly's endeavour. But Reilly is his best mate, a 'genuine mucker' is as affectionate a term as the rough patter yields.

The worlds of the buses and the family, which are set out in alternate sections in the first chapter, are briefly brought together in the second. It is Saturday night, and Hines's crowd (including the two who had a brawl) and their partners meet in a pub. When Rab and Sandra enter they find the women seated at one table, the men at another – a segregation, but probably also an ambience, which Sandra deeply resents, as Hines becomes painfully aware. It is one of several instances that bring the tensions between the two into the open.

What weighs on their relationship are not primarily the unsocial work shifts of his job, though they undoubtedly put stress on the marriage, but Hines's lack of worldly ambition. A wretched timekeeper, he has been barred from entering the busdriving school. But his bad record is itself the result of an inextricable mix of recklessness, recalcitrance and dislike of the job. He is 'sick of this eternal busconducting' (p. 39), yet cannot think of any real alternative, except the dole. Aware that '1-man buses are the vehicular items of the not too distant future' (p. 80), he occasionally contemplates emigrating, like his brother, to Australia, but it is little more than a pipe dream. Then there is the principled ethical side to his professional inertia, which comes out in the final showdown with the transport authorities over his adamant refusal to accept a formal admonition, dressed in full uniform, outside his working hours. It seems a trivial point, but Hines is incensed by the petty bureaucracy and has a sharp eye for social inequality: 'Would you sit there talking to me if you werent getting paid for it?' (p. 210), he questions the desk clerk. He also baffles union officials by speaking out against wage differentials between conductors, drivers and inspectors, and objects to the shop steward patronizingly being addressed by his first name ('They let Sammy go down to speak and he will address McGilvaray as Mr and in return be addressed as Sammy' [p. 203]). Hines the leveller simply cannot keep his mouth shut. The majority of the workforce, those to whom he sometimes refers as 'idiots', would have been cowed had they been in his skin. Not so Hines. He leads an ordinary life, but he is not an ordinary character. His shedding of the patriarchal role is exemplary, the courage of his convictions admirable, his articulate powers formidable.

For Sandra, however, a part-time office worker, brought up in comfortably middle-class Knightsbridge and looking back on a five-year marriage without marked social improvement, the accumulated strain proves too much. The upwardly mobile aspirations of her parents, carefully accentuated, have led her to expect more from life. 'She looked for him to do something. Yet if she had worked things out she would have recognized the extent of the choice. She didnt work things out. She stayed with him in the rejections but failed to see the sum as finite' (p. 103). This is the Hines who is resigned to his fate and rather self-righteously allocates the blame to the dark powers that be, the conspiracies of chance, the congeries of irritations thrown in his way.

'What is wrong with Hines, then? I'm not sure, and neither is he,' an exasperated early reviewer asked.[2] The key lies in the specific mode of working of the bus conductor. Hines is perpetually in motion, yet paradoxically making no headway. Nor is he the master of his own movements. For Cairns Craig, this absurd situation, as absurd as Sisyphus's rolling of the rock, constitutes a true 'allegory of being': 'The Busconductor is the time-keeper of the world's journeys, but he himself journeys nowhere, travelling out only to come back, travelling forwards only to reach a terminus which is no conclusion. The Busconductor is an emblem of modernity: a world structured by endless restless travel, an existence dominated by time.'[3]

This unceasing to and fro connects Hines's condition with the restless, shifting characters of the early short stories, except that their peregrinations appear less repetitive and less time-bound. In fact, for a bus conductor Hines surprisingly often strides through the city. On the other hand, he has familial and social ties, even a job, if under threat, which the vagrants do not possess. The trouble is that the satisfactions he derives from these more fortunate circumstances do not, or only moderately, relieve his sufferings. There is then a tension at the heart of the novel. Kelman wants us to see that the situation Hines finds himself in is 'a class thing': 'Somebody like Hines doesn't have any choice. He's not on the broo because he's a masochist – or on the buses because he *wants* to be on the buses.'[4] In other words, he is trapped by his class background, and especially his situation as a lowly-paid, unskilled worker. And this – the classic naturalist – version Hines himself voices in several of his outbursts. That a proletarian childhood in Drumchapel narrowly limits a person's possibilities hardly needs explaining. Yet to what degree it determined Hines's path is unclear. As a schoolboy he showed real promise and could have got his highers. However, for some unspecified reason, much to the distress of his mother, he has accomplished nothing worth mentioning. Whereas both his brother and sister and, more importantly still, Reilly have moved, or are about to move, out of the trap, Hines makes no progress. The uncustomary contraction of 'bus' and 'conductor', which Kelman does not employ in *A Chancer* when his protagonist uses public transport, indicates the rigid fixity of Hines's condition. His life on the buses is irrevocably that of a 'busconductor'.[5]

But why is Reilly not trapped or tormented? Does not every word of Craig's assertion apply equally to a bus *driver*, a position Hines has written off? In view of his sequestered position in a cabin (in British buses), the driver would be a better emblem of the essential loneliness of modern man in existentialist thinking than the conductor, who still enjoys a modicum of communication and physical contact with the passengers. There must then be another, more fundamental, not necessarily class-grounded side to Hines's problems. Hines is driven by 'an existential awareness from which most human beings are insulated by their society . . . [He is] absurdly and gratuitously thrown into an existence which makes no sense and has no place' for him.[6] This alienated condition rather than his workplace difficulties accounts for his deep malaise, his indecision and his sense of futility. All this sets him apart from his environment and further emphasizes his outsider status. But how is one's awareness of this condition generated? How does one become an 'elect' existential self? Is it Hines's reading matter? From the start we

35

discover his wide-ranging interests and, though we are not told exactly what authors he reads, we learn on one occasion that he can converse 'on subjects of a metaphysical nature' (p. 95), on another that the three books he is studying 'covered a period of some 2,500 years and spanned three continents' (p. 163). Is he depressed and paralysed because of the widening gap between his intellectual horizon and his dead-end job? No clear explanation is offered, presumably because Kelman is more interested in the 'how' than in the 'why' of his character's predicament, whose paradoxical position is neatly summed up in the striking title of a French *chanson* of 2001: 'La vie ne vaut rien, rien ne vaut la vie.'[7]

All his nervous energy and all his frustrations are thus channelled into extraordinary cerebral acts and ventilated in verbal feats. 'Predisposed towards speculative musings' (p. 93) about the world at large and anguished by the threat to the poles of his existence, he shuts himself off and plunges into a self-consuming introspection. And it is only by imaginatively stepping outside himself that he gains the distance necessary for an ironic running commentary on his situation. This self-conscious and self-mocking stance, which enables Hines to think and speak of himself in the third person, functions simultaneously as a protective shield with which at least temporarily to fend off the encroaching despair. Here he is reluctantly getting up at a quarter-to-five on a winter morning, worried about being late for work – he has been dismissed twice before on account of various misdemeanours and already has a bad file again – and yet deeply averse to setting out in the biting frost:

> come on there you there Hines! get crunching to your fucking place of work, the poor auld punters by christ they await, they stand chittering at bleak outposts, their pitiful attempts to retain body heat while where is the blooming bus. O for fuck sake but it's freezing man can you imagine lying in your kip, the breakfast in bed and that, brought by this amazing big blonde with no knickers.
>
> Shut up ya cunt I'm going to my work.
>
> Naw but imagine it man you're lying there sound asleep, right out the game, then a wee nudge on the shoulder, eh darling, eh darling, you awake, you ready for a bit of morning fare . . .
>
> Hunch the shoulders and march. The furtively fast figure. One fine morning Hines R. was arrested. Crackle crackle crackle. We have this fantasy coming through on the line sir should we tape it and

hold it against him or what. Naw but honest sir he's just a lowly member of the transport experience; he slept in a little and perforce is obliged to walk it to work, having missed the staff bastarn omnibus. A certain irony granted but nothing more, no significance of an insurrectionary nature. (pp. 113–14)

Not only are there several voices in Hines's head, he also commands different linguistic registers, from the most colloquial and down to earth to the exceedingly elevated and formal, and it is the collision between the two that makes for the irony of this virtuoso performance. Since Hines's speech patterns including the 'bad'-language words 'fucking', 'cunt' and 'bastarn' are presented, here as elsewhere in the novel, as perfectly normal, part and parcel of the character's baggage, the more refined and formal expressions such as 'await' and 'perforce', or the circumstantial 'retain body heat', take on an outlandish quality and are debunked in the process. Especially the polysyllabic utterances 'significance' and 'insurrectionary', put into the mouth of an official, and the authority behind them, are exposed to ridicule.

It might, of course, be objected that it is not quite clear who is actually speaking in the extract. The difficulty arises from the fact that in Kelman's novels, contrary to the greater part of the stories, there is no first-person narrator. At the same time it is a measure of the success of the author's effort to obliterate in *The Busconductor Hines* the narrative voice as an outside interfering agency that the reader still feels as if there were one. So frequently are we in the mind of the protagonist, so compatible are the linguistic registers and tones of voice, so seamless is the transition from one voice to the other. 'come on there you there Hines!' This could be Hines exhorting himself, but instead of an interior monologue it might also be an ironic commentary of the narrative voice. Or the two souls dwelling in Hines's breast might be in dialogue. What can be ruled out is a dialogue between narrator and character because that would destroy the naturalist illusion: Hines is not aware of a narrator looking over his shoulder. To blur the borderlines further, there are a few instances where suddenly an 'I' voice appears (pp. 104, 213), close to, or identical with, Hines's own, and this is clearly not an authorial or editorial lapse. Whose voice there is becomes then often undecidable.

The overall effect of this narrative technique is a collusion between narrative voice and central consciousness, with the ultimate aim to provide an undeflected view of a workingman stuck in an existentialist dilemma, not to inspect it from an outside, superior angle. Inevitably, such a perspective privileges Hines's view of himself and the world, and invites our sympathy. At no point are we, for example, in Sandra's mind. We do not accompany her, as we do Hines, when she visits *her* parents. Nor are we told in any detail what she does one night when, unusually, she fails to come home until very late and Hines falls into a black mood.

The anarchic imagination of the central character is the one vibrant activity in a prevailing atmosphere of stasis and repetition. Except for the fracas at the beginning and the row over Hines's failure to turn up for work towards the end, incident is sparse. But the minimalism of incident does not spell an absence of drama, only it is the drama of everyday life. Hines may lose his wife, 'the 3 of them, the trio of persons sir the 1, the unit, that impetus for continued survival' (p. 93) may break up. Despite a moving reconciliation and lovemaking after Sandra's late homecoming, the nagging uncertainties remain. And he may get the boot. At the end of the novel it is work as usual for Hines, with the issue of his dismissal in the balance. Just as a domestic and a workplace scene frame the novel, so Hines keeps on zigzagging between home and the buses. It is the unnerving insecurity, the threat of loss, not the actual onset of the disaster itself, that causes the desperation – a desperation that at one point makes him think of suicide.

In its exclusive focus on the protagonist, *A Chancer* (1985) resembles its predecessor. But in one respect the narrative mode is rather different:

> He was standing at the corner opposite where the convoy of buses would leave. People were already filing aboard or having their luggage loaded into the rear compartments by the drivers. Ten minutes from time and still they had not appeared, then he saw them. They came from Buchanan Street, running across Sauchiehall Street, suitcases and holdall bags swinging and both Rab and Donnie were carrying large carry-out bags. John and Billy were first aboard. The bus driver was chatting to Rab and then with Donnie the three of them stepped away from the rear and began to look this way and

that way but finally they stepped up inside the bus. A few minutes later the first of the convoy moved out from the stance. Tammas edged a little farther back down the lane and he turned aside while their bus passed. (p. 56)

Tammas watches his friends go off on a weekend excursion to Blackpool, from which he is pulling out at the last moment because he has lost all his money in a betting shop. It is a sad and disturbing scene, but one can only assume that he is bound to be miserable, for his interior remains sealed off. The narrative reports the event from the outside, in a low-key, matter-of-fact, unemotional manner, and to that extent it is 'objective'. Its 'subjectivity' derives from the chosen vantage point, which is close to Tammas's. And it stays hard on his heels throughout the novel, though it rarely gives us access to his mind and feelings other than through dialogue, of which there is consequently a much larger amount than in *The Busconductor Hines*.

This restrained technique, difficult enough to sustain and not deployed again in the later fiction, may be owed to the early date of composition of the novel. Its origins lie before *The Busconductor Hines*, in the phase when Kelman was still experimenting with his short stories. This proximity also explains the overlap of settings. The factory, the bedsit, the pub, the betting shop, the domino table, the snooker hall are familiar territory; to which are added here the greyhound stadium, the race track, the casino and the gambling club.

The latter locales have a special relevance, for Tammas has come to the conclusion that betting and gambling offer him as sound a chance as any to fill up his days and exert some kind of control over his life. To the consternation of his workmates and his sister and brother-in-law with whom he boards, he chucks his dead-end job in a factory – rumours of redundancies are in the air anyway – and lives henceforth on his weekly giro and the proceeds from his wins, whenever there are any.

This is another case of distinct job allergy, a constant in Kelman's world. Hines walked out before being dismissed, although out of consideration for the family he subsequently retracted. Patrick Doyle, the disaffected teacher, one afternoon simply does not return to the classroom, end of story. Sammy Samuels in *How Late it Was, How Late* has been in out and out of work, in and out of prison, all his adolescent and adult life.

Professional pride is no longer on the agenda. For Tammas, the youngest of the protagonists, the only relief from the unmitigated necessity of work is provided by the company of his workmates and the workpauses, in which we typically find him playing cards for money. To turn to gambling is thus an escape, a flight from necessity. As it turns out, he does not fare worse after having handed in his notice, and his life does not substantially alter. He stays in his digs, keeps the same friends and his financial situation alternates as before between being 'skint' and having cash. He takes a taxi whenever he has backed a winner, knowing full well that a couple of days later he may not even be able to afford boarding a bus. Now he will, in his natural generosity, treat his mates to rounds of beer and even hand out a betting ticket, the next moment he has to raid the meter bowl at home to get some fags. Money, when available, is there to be spent: on smoke, drink and grub. But its possession carries no value in itself, it is in no way a means of buying status, security, a home or family. Tammas's haphazard lifestyle may be the feckless demeanour of a 20-year old; but it is as much the age-old plebeian habit of immediate gratification, which already baffled eighteenth-century middle-class observers of 'the poor'.

The text graphically marks out Tammas's obsession with horses and dogs by frequently using Arabic numerals. These figures leap to the reader's eye:

> Something was up. He continued on and into the bar but then he about turned and raced back to the bookie and took the 16/1 to £1.50.
> At the bar he hesitated before ordering a bottle of beer. The more he thought about it the more he knew he was right. Rimini was the one and that was that. All along he had been expecting 8/1 and hoping to catch 10's with a wee bit of luck. Now he was with 16/1 and reneging – just having a safe £1.50. A price like 16/1 was wrong. And the favourite was definitely a bad bet at 7/4. If Rimini was trying then – Christ; all it needed was it to be trying and it was a certainty.
> He struck a match and lighted a cigarette while striding back outside. There was no 16's to be had. He strode along each row but nothing, and now 12/1 seemed the best on offer. And away along to where he had taken the 14/1 the bookie was offering 10's. 10's! Tammas turned and raced back down the row and grabbed the first 12/1 he could get about his remaining £5.   (p. 119)

Facts and figures, unremittingly detailed, are important means for Kelman in establishing the reality of his characters.[8] The free indirect discourse lists the odds in detail because Tammas is completely engrossed in them. The excitement of these moments is so intense that it occasionally bursts into the open through a subdued form of interior monologue.

The figures are, of course, all about money, or the prospect of it. In Kelman's texts there are constant reminders of how much cash a character has got left ('his remaining £5'), when the next giro is due, or bills have to be paid. The source of every pound they spend is named. Dividends, unexpected incomes or inheritances are unheard of. Financial security is such a distant possibility as to be totally unreal. The accumulated savings of Hines and his wife amount to the princely sum of £80, Tammas at first has none, though later he opens a deposit account after a big win.

As abstract mathematical numbers, the stakes represent also the utter irrationality of the betting system. For a slip of paper, the receipt for his bet, Tammas may suddenly obtain an amount of cash, for which in the factory he would have to drudge for months, and the whole bargain legitimized by a state that fattens itself on the resulting tax. Tammas does study the form of the racehorses or greyhounds in the sports papers, but when all is said and done favourites lose as often as they win, which is why he takes the results philosophically. 'He had £1.50 in his pocket and it had come from nothing, and that was the only point' (p. 62).

On yet another level, betting is also a cipher for the universe Tammas inhabits. For people like him, life is a spinning wheel with the odds generally staked against them. The randomness of wins and losses reflects the fortuitousness of these existences. Cairns Craig sees here another enactment of the basic existential condition,[9] though Tammas does not appear to share Hines's awareness of it. He is as discontented as anybody else in this austere world of single-ends (Vi's flat), where a telephone or bathroom is a luxury article, but he cannot be said to suffer from existential anguish. Although another book-reader, he is simply too young, too naïve, too inexperienced.

As Tammas graduates from factory to casino, from cards to chips, one catches oneself wishing, against one's better judgement, that when he is on top he will for once pocket the proceeds and do away with his all-consuming gambling mania.

The reason for this sympathy is that, though Tammas is not nearly so articulate or humorous as Hines, Kelman manages to portray him with equal compassion. Tammas can be awkward, diffident and withdrawn, but he is also possessed of human decency and generosity. He behaves irresponsibly towards his sister, who worries her head off when he stays away for several nights without a word. He lets his mates down when they have planned the weekend in Blackpool. But these weaknesses, in part owed to his immaturity, are in the end harmless, and he makes up for them through his liberality. He is also capable of learning a lesson or two, quite apart from the stock-in-trade of gambling. Early on he deserts his girlfriend as they are going to the pictures since it hurts his male pride that he cannot pay. When the occasion arises again, this time in his spasmodic relationship with Vi, a single mother, he squirms but accepts that she buys the tickets. It is a small thing, but in this spartan picture it is the small gestures, the sudden frowns, the laconic statements, even Tammas's consonantic utterances, his 'Hh's, that matter. 'What're you fucking hhing at ya bastard?' (p. 197), an irritated mate asks him.

Striking up with resourceful independent Vi brings out Tammas's most engaging characteristics. For the first time he is stirred out of his boredom. Suddenly we notice how vulnerable he is – a trait submerged under the rough-and-tumble camaraderie of his environment. He is taken aback when called a chancer only because he raised his age when he met the older Vi. He is full of self-reproach when shown the door. He is affectionate to both Vi and the baby girl, though again at one stage he just vanishes. Here, as in his other escapades, it is vaguely suggested that being stony broke may account for his temporary seclusion, for once he is back on the winning side he reappears on the scene with presents.

Again, one finds oneself hoping quite in vain that the relationship may last; for Vi's sake too, since she lives under the threat of a violent husband currently in jail. Crime and violence are hinted at in the novel, but never allowed to occupy the centre-stage. They breed in a social climate of menial jobs and growing unemployment, hopelessness and apathy, but that Tammas steers clear of them makes him all the more likeable. He is not tempted into the break-in proposed by a friend, and rightly grows indignant at his brother-in-law's insinuation that all may not be quite kosher with his sporadic big spendings.

The Busconductor Hines was divided into numbered chapters, suggesting some kind of progression over the four weeks or so that we follow Hines's vagaries. *A Chancer* is temporally more indefinite. The various episodes are separated by dots, and the narrative makes it impossible to tell how much time has passed between them. There is Christmas and Hogmanay all right, and several of Tammas's friends quit Glasgow over what must be a period of months. But it is all one for him, his fortunes see-saw continually up and down. So development is again minimal, and in terms of incident the story is even more of a non-event than the preceding one.

Tammas turns in circles – between his bedroom, Simpson's Bar, the betting shop, Ayr raceground, Shawfield dog track and the casino – as much as Hines does between garage, terminus and home. Now and then there lurks the chance to break out of the circle. A friend gets him a job in a copper-rolling factory. But this turns out to be such hard and dangerous work that, like the warehouseman or the sweeper-up in the short stories, Tammas cannot stand it for more than half a day, especially after he hears that his bets laid during the teabreak have won him a fortune. Not for him a humdrum life of ill-paid drudgery. He favours outdoor work, which is as well, because of the rumoured big pay packets of North Sea oil, which lure people away from Glasgow. Fed up with being lectured by his brother-in-law or older neighbours and intent on getting around, he considers working on a building site near Peterhead. He has the example of his friends who have moved south to Hull and Manchester or as far away as New Zealand, for, as one of them declared outright: 'This place is dead Tammas you've got to admit it' (p. 168).

In the end he hitches a lift, not to Peterhead, but to London. In one sense he has therefore burnt his boats, and though any such change of place contains the flicker of a new start, whether he can rid himself of his congenital gambling is another matter. Kelman is not one for facile optimism, but a sense of untapped human potential is implied at the end. In an interview he has called Tammas 'a trier'.[10] The ending was anticipated by the departure of one mate after another. And the unspent energy that needs an outlet is symbolized by the many runs into which

Tammas breaks, often for no ostensible reason.

These and other scenes are reminiscent of the fidgety movements of the unemployed adolescent youths in Ken Loach's film *Looks and Smiles* (1981), from a Barry Hines script, which records the first blows of the recession as they hit school-leavers, and particularly the males, in the north of England, and traces how their confidence is undermined and traditional gender roles are eroded. The picture-going episode in Kelman's novel provided one such example. Loach's film has an identical scene.

The novel is not concerned with either Tammas's future or his past. In *The Busconductor Hines* we caught glimpses of the protagonist's childhood; *A Chancer* affords no such retrospective glances. On one occasion Tammas visits his grandmother in a nursing home, but there is no mention of his parents, let alone his schooling. We are forever in the present, a present over which there hangs a stifling air of despondency relieved only in the intensely felt moments of betting and the togetherness with Vi.

Can this aspect of the novel be read as a subliminal metaphor for the state of Scotland after the onslaught of deindustrialization and the failed referendum of 1979? A city (and, by implication, a country) whose ubiquitous colour is grey, whose inhospitable climate (both novels are set in winter) is uninviting, whose frustrated sons must emigrate to secure a decent living and whose resounding keynote is stagnation – all that seems to reflect a prevalent mood of the 1980s. And one could marshall other West of Scotland writers, from William McIlvanney to Alasdair Gray and Agnes Owens, for supporting evidence. But, just as the numbing despondency gave way, not least through the cultural resurgence in which these writers played a prominent role, to a defiant new confidence with which to tackle Scotland's economic and political problems, so the bleakness of Kelman's first two novels is offset by the vitality of the language and Hines's irrepressible humour. Already in *The Busconductor Hines* the impression of unilateral pessimism in the representation of Glasgow was qualified by the recurrent phrase 'this grey but gold city' or indeed once 'grey but gold country' (p. 95). This pointer to the resources of hope beneath an oppressive everyday reality is to be found in all the above-mentioned writers.

4

Authority Flouted: The Plays and Essays

As early as 1978 Kelman had a play broadcast by BBC Radio
Scotland entitled *Hardie and Baird: The Last Days*. Given the
author's fine ear for dialogue and the importance of voice in his
fiction, the attraction of the dramatic form comes as no surprise.
Yet the technical demands of radio drama or the theatre are
naturally very different from those of fiction. Impossible here,
for example, to retain the merging of narrative and character
voice that dominates the stories and novels. Nor does the
minimalism of dramatic event in the fiction easily lend itself to
stage adaptation, even though there are instances of a similar
paucity of action in post-1945 drama.

Of the three plays collected in *Hardie and Baird & Other Plays*
(1991), one is based on a short story and treats a similar footloose
incident, but the other two are more overtly political works. *In
the Night* thematizes harassment by the secret police, which
foreshadows the later novel *Translated Accounts*, while the title
play is an excursion into Scotland's radical history, which has no
equivalent whatsoever in the fiction. To look for a common
denominator of these three plays is to risk forcing the material
into an artificial frame, but this much can be said: the principal
characters lead lives that are on the edge. The three streetwalk-
ers in *The Busker* live from hand to mouth. The unmarried couple
in *In the Night* are involved in left-wing political activities, and
the title figures of *Hardie and Baird* are incarcerated rebels
awaiting execution. In one way or another they have all fallen
foul of authority.

A spin-off from 'Old Holborn', one of the *Lean Tales*, *The Busker* (1985), reworks and extends the same material. The story is told from the perspective of a vagrant who approaches a street guitarist with the evident hope of taking a cut. He gives the impression of improving the earnings by doing the collecting, but the musician sees through his game and does not appreciate his aggressive accosting of the pedestrians. Still, the first-person narrator who claims not to have eaten anything for days feels that he is due something, and he manages to scrounge a pound, half the takings, off the generous busker. Then he disappears with an easy conscience.

This action has gone straight into the play, but it covers no more than the first act. Acts II and III develop the relationship through the cadger's return and the introduction of a third character, a 'Lady'.

But the differences between the two genres can already be discerned in Act I. They result in the first place from the shifting of perspectives in the dialogue. The speaker-narrator of 'Old Holborn' gives his own version of the encounter, in which he plays down his parasitic behaviour. In *The Busker* the sympathies of the audience are directed towards the musician, and for the reader of the play the distribution of roles is even more clearly marked by naming the characters Busker and Ponce. Other differences include the location, which in the story is left deliberately vague but in the play is firmly set on a Birmingham pavement, and the elaboration of the pun on 'Old Holborn', which is not the London district, as the Cockney voice of the Busker may lead one to believe, but the tobacco from which he rolls his cigarettes.

The regional identities are ironically exploited through the voices. The Ponce is a 'Jock', and nothing irritates him more than the discovery that the assumed Cockney suddenly falls into a Glaswegian patter:

> How come ye lay on the Cockney accent? . . .
>
> D'you hear that? Still calling me jock, same as the English. What d'you make of that! Imagine calling your fellow countryman jock! (Act II, pp. 36, 39).

For the Busker this is one way of getting his own back after having been tapped for cigarettes and money. All he wants is to be left alone:

> Listen, I'm here trying to earn, right? I'm trying to earn, I'm trying to
> get a few quid, I mean this is my living. I'm a busker, I'm a fucking
> busker. I get paid dough for playing some music . . . . I'm no here for
> a fucking party, know what I mean! (Act II, p. 35).

This is after the 'Lady', itself an ironical naming, has arrived on
the scene. Her entry generates a new dynamic as alliances are
now constantly formed and abandoned. Only a threesome
allows for such a shifting configuration, and her ambivalent
behaviour, now siding with the one, then with the other, amply
bears out a statement by the author that women, though absent
from the early short stories, structurally play an important role
in the longer works.[1] The protagonists' relationships with
Sandra in *The Busconductor Hines* and Vi in *A Chancer* helped to
bring out the emotional, tender, unprotected side of their
characters, and the same is true of the gender relations in the
later novels. In the play the Lady's fainting makes the two
antagonists forget their squabble, as both are attentive to her
needs, though the Busker a trace 'more knowledgeably' (Act III,
p. 42). If this is the most dramatic incident in *The Busker*, it
typically happens between the acts, so as not to allow it to
become too stagey.

Dramatization, then, is low key. It relies on shifting relationships, the raising of the voices, verbal violence, the threatening
gesture. The possibility of a street brawl is intimated, but not
realized. As might be expected from reading the stories, Kelman
neither idealizes nor condemns these footloose figures. Each of
them is by turns on his guard, playing games, ironical, touchy,
hurt and angry. There is nothing forced about such behaviour
given the context of a casual encounter. In their individual ways
each is shown to be preoccupied with immediate and concrete
ends of a material kind: securing a modest living through street
music, chumming up for the sole purpose of survival, taking a
break from some undefined business (the Lady who is suddenly
in a hurry 'to go a message' (Act III, p. 50)).[2]

Whereas *The Busker* operates unequivocally on a realist level,
Kelman's next play *In the Night* (1987) defies easy classification. It
has a realist side captured by the blurb's designation of it as a
'chilling drama'. But there is also a non-lifelike dimension in the

characters' behaviour and exchanges, which is what the author may have had in mind when he referred to it as 'satire'.[3]

At dawn three officials burst into a couple's flat and commence interrogation. They bully, sneer and fabricate vague charges (atheism, disrespect for the family in general and the royals in particular, unconstitutional behaviour) from their own prejudices about unmarried relationships, the Irish or any conceivable 'Other', all the time keeping their victims standing naked, covered only with blankets. This humiliating practice of extorting confessions is the sinister, 'night'marish side of the situation. There is no use of brute force or torture, though the menace of it ('A lesson of the short and sharp variety' [Act II, p. 95]) is upheld whenever the tension is slackening.

As in *The Busker*, the characters are unnamed, simply identified as Man and Woman; First, Second (a female who appears to be in command) and Third Inter. The latter term used for the agents suggests anything from interrupt, interfere, intercept to, more ominously, interrogate and, as a possible destiny, intern. Although there are references to Britain, Kelman universalizes the situation by keeping the participants anonymous, as in the later novel *Translated Accounts*. Detainees do not learn the names of their interrogators or torturers, and to the agents they are faceless suspects, guilty of crimes against the established order.

But from the start there are also a number of 'surreal' elements in the play. Even before the First Inter breaks in, the Man pictures, or dreams, the invasion that follows, and it is never made quite clear whether the whole scenario may not merely be a figment of his imagination, or an actual nightmare from which he might awake at any moment. Although there is nothing at the end to support the idea of a framing device, the unreality of it all is hinted at again, at a later stage, when he has the impression of taking part 'in a picture, or a story . . . You hear this voice, the narrator, talking about me as if I was the real character' (Act I, p. 77).

Is this the reason why the couple do not appear surprised to be apprehended in such a manner, and why the intruders feel no necessity to explain their presence? More strangely still, the Inters converse amongst themselves, and display signs of disagreement and uncertainty.

The satire lies in the stock phrases and thinking of the

security officials, predictable to the point of caricature. Non-conformist political views and sexual mores are suspect because they represent something 'distinctly unwholesome', 'unhealthy' (Act I, p. 75). This in turn suggests a tendency to political extremism, primarily represented by Ireland. But if it is not the IRA, it is another foreign brand, Communism. 'You are both subversive elements, you are radical left-wing communists. Loonies . . .' (Act I, p. 80), the couple is told. There follows the insinuation that they are paid agents of 'Russia or North Pakistan. Maybe even Cuba!' (Act II, p. 96). The overarching aim of the enemies of the state is, of course, 'to bring down the government . . ., to bring about the complete destruction of our whole way of life, the actual fabric of our entire existence' (Act II, p. 95). Next, exile, the classic treatment of dissenters, is urged upon them: 'how come yous don't bloody emigrate? If you hate Great Britain so much as all that then surely yous must want to leave' (Act I, p. 80). Why don't you go to the East, was a favourite catchphrase hurled at left-wing West Germans until the 1980s.

In this mix of realism and absurdity there are echoes of Kafka and Pinter. The private room is no longer a safe haven, its promised protection gone. The entry of the stranger into the routine world of its inhabitants brings menace and victimiza-tion, though in Kelman's play we do not witness mental or physical breakdown. The Man's last word, uttered twice, is a stubborn 'No' (Act II, p. 102). He is not broken.

In his 'Notes on direction' Kelman stipulated that the 'accent of each character must be the same . . . the RP "voice" of British authority is excluded at all costs, and that there should be no class distinguishing features between the five characters' (p. 54). What are the implications of this ruling? Is it further evidence that the voices of the Inters exist only in the Man's head, a projection of his innermost fears? Is it to indicate that the repressive state organs recruit their personnel from amongst ordinary citizens? Is it the suggestion that victimizer and victimized, hunter and hunted, are bound up in a ritualized power game? So much remains mysterious in this play that it is perhaps no wonder that the first production at Battersea Arts Centre in March 1987 'bore little resemblance to the play' Kelman felt he had written (p. 53).

No such ambivalences are present in *Hardie and Baird: The Last*

Days (1990), the play about an incident in Scottish social history known, if remembered at all, as the Weavers' Rebellion or the Battle of Bonnymuir of 1820, in which a small band of radicals, misled by the assumption of an imminent general rising in Britain and possibly incited by an agent provocateur, attempted to claim their lost birthright ('annual Parliaments and Election by ballot' [Act I, Sc. 13, p. 150]) by armed force.[4] The twenty-odd insurrectionaries, a mere tenth of the expected turnout, were quickly overwhelmed by the military and faced a charge of high treason. Their two leaders Andrew Hardie and John Baird, voted into that position on the strength of their experience as soldiers in the Napoleonic Wars, were held in solitary confinement and subjected to the full severity of the law, which included hanging, beheading and quartering, while the sentences of the others were commuted.

Kelman's play is not primarily a plea against capital punishment, as was the case with the prison literature of Jean Genet (*Le condamné à mort*, 1942) and Brendan Behan (*The Quare Fellow*, 1956), written at a time when most European countries were still executing criminals. The Prologue makes clear that it is rather part of an ongoing reclamation of a forgotten chapter of Scottish history:

> Neither the two men nor the Scottish Insurrection in general are ever referred to officially, while within our educational system this part of history, like so many others connected with the Radical movement, remains almost entirely neglected.
>
> In the year 1820 there were eighty-eight counts of High Treason in Scotland. There were many transportations and three weavers were executed: James 'Purly' Wilson at Glasgow; John Baird and Andrew Hardie at Stirling. The trials themselves were held under English Law, in direct contravention of the 1707 Treaty of Union. (p. 109)

It is thus fitting and entirely in keeping with our earlier remarks about low-key dramatization that there is no scaffold or skirmish scene in the play. Kelman focuses instead on the term spent by the two radicals in the dungeons of Edinburgh and Stirling castles where they were awaiting trial and finally execution. How can such a play show the prisoners coping with solitary confinement and yet demonstrate their common fate? Kelman's answer was to have both cells on the stage throughout the long first act. The movements and utterances of the two men can thus be followed by the audience, though not by each other.

As always in Kelman, we find that the lower-class characters are literate and articulate individuals, even given the historical setting of the play. It opens with Hardie engrossed in writing a letter and, a little later, reading the Bible. Their abject conditions are brought out: damp cells, cold food, no visits from friends or relatives,[5] no correspondence (letters have to be smuggled out), no exercise in the prison yard, initially no reading matter other than the Bible. Both draw inspiration from comparing their lot with that of other radicals languishing in prison: Thomas Muir in the 1790s, Dr Dodd, and James Wilson, the leader of the contemporaneous Strathaven Rising, who was also sentenced to death.

And yet these two men, who had not met until the fatal day of the insurrection, are very different characters. Baird emerges as the dour realist, defiant to the end, refusing to speak to minister or gaoler, with no illusions about the rulers of the country. As in Shelley's revolutionary poetry from the year 1819, Castlereagh and Sidmouth are singled out as tyrants: 'They've never gave us nothing wioot it being wrested from them, never. We've aye had to fight. Every bit o progress, it's had to get tore aff them, they'd have gave us nothing if we'd left it to them – nothing' (Act II, Sc. 6, p. 180). These are among his last words. But he is not without a sensitive side. He has, for example, fond memories of a sweetheart in England, by whom he may have a son now aged 10.

By contrast, Hardie is a deeply religious man, who abhors Baird's and the gaoler's swearing and blaspheming, finds consolation in the Scripture and derives his political standpoint from it: 'Equality exists in the Bible and must exist in the state' (Act II, Sc. 1, p. 165). Whereas Baird in his disgust at the 'state-paid clergy' (Act II, Sc. 4, p. 171) demonstratively turns his back on the three ministers visiting them, Hardie (and with him Kelman) is careful to distinguish between the two smugly speaking representatives of the Church and the more thought-ful Mr Heugh, who cannot conceal his sympathies for the two men, if not for their action, and thanks to whom they obtain books. Baird smells betrayal in his comrade's more open-minded stance to the visiting clergy: 'What right have they got to tell us to repent? I've nothing to repent for ken nothing.

51

I've done nothing I'm ashamed of. On the one hand you say everything we done was for justice, freedom and truth – for aw that we believe in and haud sacred – the next thing ye turn roon and start to repent. Repent! For what?' (Act II, Sc. 4, p. 171). But Hardie does not recant on his politics: 'I'm no repenting for marching. I'm no ashamed of nothing we done. It's just that we're aw sinners' (Act II, Sc. 4, p. 172). Repenting is for him generally incumbent on the position of Man in a 'whole sinful world' (Act II, Sc. 4, p. 173). And he is, above all, concerned to counter the propaganda and lies spread by the authorities about their action, and to leave to posterity an account of their true motives:[6] 'I took up arms not to rob or plunder, but for the restoration of these rights for which our forefathers bled and which we have allowed shamefully to be wrested from us and I trust the innocent blood that is soon to be shed will awaken my countrymen from that lethargy which has so overcrowded them' (Act II, Sc. 5, p. 174).

Kelman is alert to a major contradiction in these men's lives when he makes Baird reflect that at Bonnymuir they were opposing the same ruling aristocracy which as British soldiers they had helped to keep in the saddle: 'For the past twenty year we've been destroying liberty wherever we find it, right across Europe – Italy, France, Germany, Spain – sticking tyrants into power. Ye wouldni credit it, wherever we find freedom we fucking destroy it. Just fucking goats so we ur, a herd of fucking goats!' (Act II, Sc. 1, p. 163). At the same time, it is interesting to observe that it required experienced and disillusioned, if still young, war veterans to lead the men into action.

In retrospect it is always easy to deride an isolated and abortive rebellion as a pathetic and naïve endeavour. But Kelman movingly and unambiguously speaks up for these determined and courageous men, imagining and, as far as possible, faithfully recreating their motivations and attitudes. In the Prologue he may have underrated the inspiration their example set to later reformers and working-class leaders.

These three published plays have not been the author's only excursions into theatre. He followed them up with One, Two – Hey! (1994), featuring the Blues Poets band, and a radio play, The Art of the Big Bass Drum, broadcast by BBC Radio 3 in 1998, of which there is, as is the case of The Busker, also a story version.[7]

Both *Hardie and Baird* and *One, Two – Hey!* had been mounted at the Traverse Theatre, Edinburgh, a subsidized house, about whose 'battling to stage "unsponsorable" work' Kelman had written appreciatively in the foreword to the plays' volume (p. 3). He was all the more incensed therefore in 1999 at the Traverse's objection to let him use their space again for the production of a new play – unless he submitted it for prior auditioning. Like *One, Two – Hey!*, this was to have been done on a 'profit-share base', Kelman arriving with his own troupe, hence at no cost to the hosting institution for actors, director, stage props, etc. Kelman adamantly refused to oblige, fulminating against the apparatchiks in the Theatre and the Scottish Arts Council as a public funding body in general.[8]

'Kelman Embattled' could serve as a blanket title for his two volumes of essays, talks and polemics, *Some Recent Attacks* (1992) and *'And the Judges Said . . .'* (2002), the latter of which is a very substantial effort of nearly 500 pages. 'Attacks' has a double-edged meaning, as the full titles of two of these essays make clear: 'Some Recent Attacks on the Rights of the People' and 'A Brief Note on the War Being Waged by the State against the Victims of Asbestos'. So, while not free from vitriol and rant ('Shouting at the Edinburgh Fringe Forum' is the title of a piece from *Judges*), these essays are as much spirited defences of civic rights as attacks on those who wield power. A zeal for justice runs through these essays and, simultaneously, a deep distrust of the judicial system in Britain. Since the 'Judges' – the title stems from a Tom Leonard poem[9] – have failed to deliver justice, Kelman feels impelled to act in an almost Romantic vein, not as an 'unacknowledged legislator', but as a judge of judges, a fearless adjudicator, whose principles are ethical rather than strictly legal ones.

For Kelman readers and critics, the importance of these essays is fourfold: they illuminate the astonishing extent of the author's practical support for the victims of political and bureaucratic ill-treatment, in particular widespread racism; they outline his working-class libertarian-socialist concerns (each of the adjectives counts); they can be tapped for a better understanding of his aesthetics; and, last but not least, they can be read as autobiography, an invaluable source for many scenes in his fiction and the writers from which he has drawn inspiration.

To start with the first point, there are not many authors of Kelman's stature in Britain today who have so consistently taken time off their work in order to become involved in campaigns, addressing meetings, sitting on panels, taking part in benefit nights, writing articles for the press, demonstrating in the streets, accompanying deputations to the powers that be – with the usual thanks of being treated as part of a bunch of 'misfits, dilettanti, well-heeled authors and critics; professional whingers, crypto-communists, self proclaimed anarchists, trotskyists' (*Attacks*, p. 3). The number of campaigns to which Kelman has lent his voice is impressive. If we consider those from the 1990s alone, there were the moves to resist the closure of the Ravenscraig steel plant; the Free University Network, which staged the 'Self-Determination and Power Event'; the Workers' City, as an antidote to the Merchant City image of Glasgow during the European City of Culture Year; the opposition to the closing-down of a Citizens' Rights Office; addresses to the Friends of Kurdistan, the Friends of Palestine and the European Action for Racial Equality and Social Justice; several appearances for Amnesty International, including a Freedom of Expression Rally in Istanbul; the Stephen Lawrence Family Campaign; the People's Tribunal on Racial Violence and Harassment, which he chaired. This is enough to occupy a person at least half-time, though the list is not even complete. Not all of these were lost causes, such as the fight for the survival of the steel industry in Scotland. But even the small victories recorded here such as out-of-court settlements for victims of asbestosis leave a bitter aftertaste, not only because of the shabby protracted negotiations over compensation for people in various stages of dying, but because 'Justice Is Not Money' (*Judges*).

Kelman's dedicated work on behalf of Clydeside Action on Asbestos, documented in three contributions, is perhaps the most heart-rending story. He cites the case of ex-shipyard worker Pat McCrystal of whose ordeal millions of television viewers became aware during a BBC Newsnight programme. McCrystal, suffering from the terminal disease mesothelioma, baffled the legal profession by stubbornly refusing cash payment. He pressed for justice, he wanted the employers who had knowingly let their workforce labour in poisonous surroundings to stand trial. It is part of the tragedy of this determined, yet tired and dying man that he was finally pushed by his own lawyers, against his principles, into accepting a record compensation, due no doubt to the publicity surrounding his case following his TV appearance. In conversation with Kelman he spoke figuratively of a 'gun held unto my head' (*Judges*, p. 17). For Kelman, the whole out-of-court settlement, necessary though it is for the victims and their families, amounts to a buying-off, plain bribery, a travesty of justice.

> The Government and the asbestos industry and their insurers have always been happy to let us think that the fight is about money. Name your price! Here we go again, the guy is walking up to you and saying: okay I admit it – now that I've been found out. Yes, it is true, I have been killing people for years. And now I'm forced to give you a bit of bad news: you're one of them. And by the way, did your wife wash your jeans or your dungarees? If so maybe I've killed her as well. Awful sorry. What about your weans by the way, did you wash your hands before you played with them when you came home from work? Did your wee boy try on your bunnet? Pardon me. How much dough can my insurers offer you to square the account? I do not mind if you get something, that is what I pay them for. Mind you, whatever you do ask for they'll fight you tooth and nail, every step of the way, to the last breath in your body. Aye and see once you're dead, they'll fight your widow as well. (*Judges*, pp. 209–10)

Such a principled stand on justice does not *per se* rest on a libertarian-socialist premiss. What this term, which was probably coined by the French Anarchist Daniel Guérin, implies is a continuous thoroughgoing questioning of authority, a radical opposition to all forms of domination and inequality, a mistrust of centralized power and the workings of state institutions. All these can be found in Kelman's work, but nowhere are they more pointedly expressed and exemplified with greater passion than in the essays.

Anything that smacks of elitism, be it the upper-class English voice, the literary coterie or the machinations of 'experts', comes under attack. In his obsessive hatred – not too strong a word – of the metropolitan literary scene Kelman is always prone to condemn fashionable English writers wholesale. Nuanced judgements are lacking when his anger is evident, though he is perfectly capable of giving a considered opinion on the Black South African writer Alex La Guma.

This strongly anti-elitist position is more inclined to a native than a continental tradition. Kelman derives it from the Scottish Enlightenment thinkers of the eighteenth century, whose notion of Common Sense as a faculty of judgement shared by all members of humanity he finds extremely attractive. If everybody can know and discern, if all of us possess the analytic skills and reasoning to attempt an understanding of the world, the role of the intellectuals and specialists is effectually diminished. An education based on a broad, generalist and unified approach to knowledge can equip people with the skills to cut through the mystifications of self-appointed experts and challenge their controlling interest, especially in the sphere of politics. It is an engaging scenario but presupposes little Kelmans everywhere, ready to learn, dispute and challenge, and neglects the role of the media in contemporary society, elsewhere blamed for 'disinformation' and 'silences' (*Judges*, pp. 41, 65), as consensus-forgers. Ideology as a concept has no place in these pages, though it is there inherently.

In a lengthy piece Kelman fêtes Noam Chomsky, one of his heroes, not least in his role as a scourge of US foreign policy, as the most prominent contemporary exponent of this Common Sense tradition. Chomsky and Kelman share a libertarian outlook, which shows, for example, in their vehement opposition to any form of censorship. In Chomsky's case this unlimited freedom of expression includes the right to disseminate lies about the Holocaust. Kelman, if pressed, would probably tolerate racist propaganda, though he would immediately add that the real problem was propaganda not by word, but by deed, that racism was an endemic feature in the public services and society at large. He quotes the huge figure of 140,000 racist assaults in Britain per year (*Judges*, p. 375).

However, there are also differences between the two. Chomsky is the analyst, the speaker to large audiences around the globe, the prolific polemicist; Kelman, the activist, a public figure *and* a man of his community, the conscientious practitioner of the craft of fiction (more reckless in his essay writing). Further, Kelman's brand of libertarianism has a socialist bent that Chomsky, for all his Jewish communist upbringing, his savage indictment of the terrorism perpetrated by the United States on its Latin American neighbours and his patent concern for the needy, does not display. 'Men can live without justice, and generally must', Eric Hobsbawm has written, 'but they cannot live without hope'.[10] That hope surfaces now and again in Kelman's essays: 'Radical change is always possible. Society can be transformed' (*Attacks*, p. 45). For Kelman, a starting-point, a first resource of hope, lies in the gaining of self-respect by (working-class and black) people into whose minds has been instilled a sense of inferiority. Once attained, such self-respect could then be built upon in the struggle for self-determination. In no way a facile optimism, this 'principle of hope' (Ernst Bloch) is an irreducible element of Socialism, and its presence in Kelman's work should not be overlooked. Kelman not only employs the socialist language of class (work, fight, struggle, solidarity, comrade, internationalism); he is always conscious of his working-class background and never oblivious of the material means on which comfort and ease are based.

It is true that Kelman's relationships with the traditional labour movement, the unions and the Labour Party are strained, to put it mildly. But to conclude, for example, from the union meeting in *The Busconductor Hines* that he generally adopts an anti-union position would be quite wrong. In 'Say Hello to John La Rose' he distinguishes between the TGWU branches he had known in the Glasgow bus depots and those on the London building sites and, true to his anti-officialdom, he makes a further distinction between the rank-and-file and the leadership:

> Through my time as an apprentice compositor I knew strong unions existed but my time with Turriff & Co revealed a more interesting point: any union at all can be strong, even those I thought a joke, such as the TGWU. They might well be a joke in general, and at the upper reaches of full-time officialdom both morally corrupt and politically bankrupt, but on the ground, the shop-floor, their strength was a function of the branches, individually and separately (as opposed to collectively which only comes later). And each branch was as strong as the commitment of the rank and file, the ordinary members. Everything hinges on that . . . . For any group engaged in struggle, success arrives from the ground, street level: even where the leadership is strong, if commitment is lacking at the bottom then problems are unavoidable, the strength is superficial, an illusion.
> (*Judges*, p. 224)

As already argued in the Introduction to this book, Kelman's anti-elitism also translates into an aesthetic position, not only with regard to the use of language but through a general validation of local and indigenous cultures. A related aspect, which emerges in these essays, is the author's hostility towards 'the endemic racism, class bias and general elitism at the English end of the Anglo American literary tradition' (*Attacks*, p. 20). This he sees embodied in 'literary totems like Rudyard Kipling, T. S. Eliot, Joseph Conrad, Evelyn Waugh, Henry James and so on' (p. 22). A reference to Chinua Achebe's startling attack on Conrad's *Heart of Darkness* was to be expected in this context.

However, more significant is Kelman's own wide reading in extra-European and -American literatures. Quite typically, he will therefore, in a balanced discussion of Salman Rushdie's *The Satanic Verses*, draw attention to the plight of lesser-known, but no less threatened and, in his view, no less important writers such as Sadaat Hasan Manto who wrote in Urdu. Kelman's appreciation of Alex La Guma has already been mentioned, but it required courage to attend an Arts and Culture Conference hosted by the ANC in Johannesburg at a time (early 1993) when safety could not be guaranteed even under escort. The Okot p'Bitek poem in *A Disaffection* belongs in this context, and so does the old African proverb 'Unity chops elephants', which serves as a motto for the *Judges* volume.

What attracted Kelman to these African or, for that matter, Caribbean writers was the kindred approach they had chosen:

> Although using the English language, these writers were NOT working to assimilate their own cultural experience within standard prose form which is possible only through ultimate surrender. Surrender was the last thing on their mind. They were attacking and the attack was formal and methodical;. . . coming on these other English-language writers from other marginalised cultures reinforced the position, speaking personally, and helped clarify the situation. (*Judges*, p. 227)

Hand in hand with this discovery went the realization that in these literary and visual cultures art and politics were interwoven to an extent unheard of in Britain and that, given the colonial and postcolonial situation, for them to have a keen political edge no immediate political subject matter was required.

By far the longest essay in *Judges* is reserved for Kafka, Kelman's revered master. His placing of Kafka in an existential tradition, ranging from Kierkegaard and Dostoevski to Camus and Sartre, and his claiming of the author as a realist of the first order, reveals much about Kelman's own preoccupations. Perusing this essay is in places like reading a self-characterization: 'Kafka's central characters are in conflict with any authority which seeks to impose itself on individuals by appealing to necessity in the face of what cannot be recognised as true' (p. 332). Or with regard to narrative voice: 'Kafka did attempt versions of his three novels in the "I" voice but he finished them in the third. He confines his use of first party to the short story' (p. 268). Or to the use of language: 'Simplicity had to be the method. In order to present a reality "in itself", language had to be pared of value to as great an extent as possible' (p. 332). Perhaps most intriguingly: 'Readers who regard the author's work as bleak and pessimistic perhaps are guilty of bringing their own prejudices to bear' (p. 331). This has, in fact, been my refrain throughout this study, to seize only on the desolate and disturbing aspects of Kelman's world is to misread him.

Finally, in four essays of *Judges*, strategically placed at the beginning, in the middle and at the end of the book, we get straightforward autobiography,[11] numerous details of Kelman's early life, absorbing interests and formative influences. If anyone still doubted it, here they can learn that, from the boy who delivers 'Sunday Papers' (in *Greyhound for Breakfast*) to the yarns in *Short Tales from the Night Shift*, from the union meeting at the end of *The Busconductor Hines* to the copper mill scene at the beginning of *A Chancer*, from Sammy's memories of work on London building sites in *How Late it Was, How Late* to the interviews with prisoners and persecutees in *Translated Accounts*, Kelman draws on his own experiences. Obviously that does not mean that these experiences have gone into the works unrefracted. It does mean, however, a valuation of human experience over and above cerebral work, intellectualization and rationalization, it stresses 'the primacy of the world as perceived and experienced by individual beings' (*Judges*, p. 38).

If this emphasis was derived from European existentialism, the other, equally non-English, source of inspiration was twentieth-century American realism, its language and its characters. Whether he came across it or not, Kelman would have endorsed the main points of Raymond Chandler's distinction between English and American writing styles:

> The merits of American style are less numerous than its defects and annoyances, but they are more powerful.
> It is a fluid language, like Shakespearean English, and easily takes in new words, new meanings for old words, and borrows at will and at ease from the usages of other languages . . .
> Its overtones and undertones are not stylised into a social conventional kind of subtlety which is in effect a class language . . .
> Final note – out of order – The tone quality of English speech is usually overlooked. This tone quality is infinitely variable and contributes infinite meaning. The American voice is flat, toneless, and tiresome. The English tone quality makes a thinner vocabulary and a more formalised use of language capable of infinite meanings. Its tones are of course read into written speech by association. This makes good English a class language, and that is its fatal effect. The English writer is a gentleman (or not a gentleman) first and a writer second.[12]

Kelman's roll-call of inspiring American realists includes Stephen Crane, Sherwood Anderson, Ernest Hemingway and, inevitably, the existential voice of Jack Kerouac, but also a good sprinkling of black authors (Richard Wright, Ralph Ellison, James Baldwin and Malcolm X, among others).

Such lists are always as interesting for what they contain as for what they exclude. Two glaring absences here are the Scottish novel and working-class writing. 'There were no literary models I could look to from my own culture. There was nothing whatsoever. I am not saying these models did not exist. But if they did then I could not find them' (*Judges*, p. 64). The only Scottish novelist Kelman pays tribute to is James Hogg. By contrast, Lewis Grassic Gibbon, whose attempt in *A Scots Quair* to write in a non-standard English voice should have commanded attention, is not mentioned.[13] Similarly with the working-class novel. In works of this genre 'the central characters rarely have time to tell a joke, fall in love, get drunk or visit the lavatory, although sometimes they are allowed to visit museums, libraries and art galleries, or do evening classes with a view to "bettering" themselves' (*Judges*, p. 39). Now that is simply untrue. It does not do justice to either *The Ragged Trousered Philanthropists* or James Hanley's fiction in the 1930s or the early Sillitoe, to name only a few examples from this tradition. One cannot help feeling that in his search for models Kelman was also trying to steer clear of political pieties – nationalist or socialist.

Whatever the case, Kelman's position evolved from the two strands of European existentialism and American realism, neither of which was home-grown. In his remembrances the author repeatedly refers to another influence from across the Atlantic, blues and country and western music, and its eventual merger with British rock. This has left its mark not only on a number of short stories and the novel *How Late it Was, How Late*, but more generally on the peculiar rhythm of his style,[14] not to mention the collaboration with musicians on the production of his plays *The Busker* and *One, Two – Hey!*.

One last point is of interest here, not the formative influences on Kelman's own distinctive voice, but, conversely, his immense impact on contemporary Scottish fiction. This has not been welcomed in every corner. Already in a review of *A Chancer* Douglas Dunn had expressed his unease at the publication of 'yet another Glasgow book which is single-minded in its dramatisation of working-class life' and offers a 'peculiarly one-sided picture of Glasgow'. 'Glasgow is as much a middle-class city as the home of Tammas' and at some point 'a novelist will have to try to be a bit more comprehensive as well as realistic'.[15] In 'Social Diversity and the Literary Order' Kelman heaps irony on these worries:

> It is to the credit of our home-based literary critics that they subject their own field of endeavour to the most stringent scrutiny with great relish and enthusiasm. Indeed the view is now being expressed that our contemporary literature is perhaps in a less healthy state than our conventional wisdom would have us believe, given the occasional glamour from excitable foreign sources. They argue that there is nothing *inherently* wrong with much if not most of the 'school of urban realism'; and clearly questions of this form belong to another context. Their concern is that the current preoccupation with this one community is in danger of presenting an imbalanced picture not only of our national literature but of the larger Scottish culture. This branch of our literature (for it is certainly that), initially Glasgow-based, has spread eastwards and further north. Nowadays

one confronts it as a matter of course in most every contemporary literary magazine or anthology. . . . The danger would arise from a disproportionate time being spent on its perusal; our students have these days a demanding academic syllabus. . . .

Much of our country is rural. Very many of our people earn their crust far from the madding thunder of city traffic, whether by farming the land or the seas surrounding our rugged coastline. Those areas of our contemporary Scottish society are every bit as ordinary (or extraordinary) as those pertaining to the urban underclasses. . . . might we not look for the poem devoted to the Hebridean shepherd, the dramatisation of the Minch fisherman whose life is daily at risk? (*Judges*, pp. 336–7)

5

Contacts, Tensions, Emotions:
Greyhound for Breakfast
and *The Burn*

In his study of Kafka Kelman quotes a diary entry by the author:
'"Don't you want to join us?" I was asked recently by an
acquaintance when he ran across me alone after midnight in a
coffee-house that was already almost deserted. "No, I don't," I
said.' Kelman then comments:

> Something is being shown about the creative process, about the
> making of stories, artistic possibility: Kafka has created the
> conditions for a 'story' but taken the ultimate possibility, he negates
> it. Yet, paradoxically, in so doing he has still written a story:
> extremely brief, yes, but a story in its own right and worthy of
> standing as such. Should anyone bring out an additional collection
> of his prose fiction in the future, there are a couple of 'new' pieces
> that may be discovered in his *Diaries*. (*Judges*, p. 272)

The remark shows, among other things, Kelman's keen alertness
to the vignette-type short story, examples of which he would
have come across in Hemingway's first booklet *in our time* (1924),
which is not much longer than *Short Tales from the Night Shift*. Or
if he did not see this small-press Parisian publication, he would
have noticed the same vignettes, interspersed and italicized, in
Hemingway's longer collection with the same, but capitalized
title (1925).

Greyhound for Breakfast (1987), which together with *The Burn*
represents the peak of Kelman's short-story writing, contains a
host of such 'wee' stories, ranging from the single paragraph to
a page and a half. In one of them, 'An old story', we find a
blocked creative situation equivalent to Kafka's. The possibilities

for a story are sketched, yet the story is never properly told.

> She'd been going about in this depressed state for ages so I should've known something was up. But I didnt. You dont always see what's in front of your nose. I've been sitting about the house that long. You wind up in a daze. You dont see things properly, even with the weans, the weans especially. There again but she's no wean. No now. She's a young woman. Ach, I dont want to tell this story. (p. 185)

As there are no speech marks it is not until the end of the first paragraph that the reader realizes that, for once, this is not an interior monologue but part of a conversation and that, unusually, the entire half-page story is made up of dialogue.

The story is as much about the first speaker's worries over his daughter (is she pregnant, 'an old story'?) as about the holding-back of her story. (Though it is nowhere stated explicitly, I can't help feeling that he is a male and that the 'young woman' is his daughter.) This is how the text continues:

> But you cant say that. Obviously the story has got to be told.
> Mm, aye, I know what you mean.
> Fine then.
> Mmm.
> Okay, so about your story. . .
> Aye.
> It concerns a lassie, right? And she's in this depressed state, because of her boyfriend probably – eh?
> I don't want to tell it.
> But you've got to tell it. You've got to tell it. Unless . . . if it's no really a story at all.
> Oh aye christ it's a story, don't worry about that. (p. 185)

Much as the second character coaxes the man into relating his story, the latter remains unwilling to do so. His monosyllabic replies (Mm, aye) indicate his reluctance, hesitation, perhaps even shame at what has happened, and when he is just about to admit, as in fact he already implicitly did at the end of the first paragraph, that there is something to tell, the narrative breaks off. The girl's story is withheld. By a mere glimpse we are given to understand what can only be hovered about because it is too sensitive, the first character's uneasiness, delusion, pain and self-reproach. And this is the story, not the untold misfortune of the 'lassie'.

In these miniature pieces tone of voice is of the utmost importance. Take the even shorter 'this man for fuck sake':

> This man for fuck sake it was terrible seeing him walk down the edge of the pavement. If he'd wanted litter we would've given him it. The trouble is we didn't know it at the time. So all we could do was watch his progress and infer. And even under normal circumstances this is never satisfactory: it has to be readily understood the types of difficulties we laboured under. Then that rolling manœuvre he performed while nearing the points of reference. It all looked to be going so fucking straightforward. How can you blame us? You can't, you can't fucking blame us.   (p. 116)

If in the first story the girl's father spoke falteringly, revealing in the process an unnerved character, this speaker-narrator, while also perturbed, is more loquacious, and employing the plural 'we' may be part of his attitude of self-defence. He clearly has a bad conscience. He doesn't want to take the blame for what has happened. But what *has* happened? Is it a case of misjudging a pedestrian's movements, a failure to give assistance to someone who tottered along and collapsed, or was even run over by a car? Once again, the emphasis is not on the actual incident, but on its impact on the witnesses. That the narrator shifts into an ironic stance halfway through only adds to his attempt at distancing and shielding himself, but the hilarity is forced, as can be seen from his insistent refusal to admit responsibility.[1]

However, there remains something enigmatic about this episode, and this is even truer of the bizarre 'Incident on a windswept beach':

> A man walked out of the sea one February morning dressed in a boilersuit & bunnet, and wearing a tartan scarf which had been tucked crosswise under each oxter to be fastened by a safety-pin at a point roughly centre of his shoulder blades; from his neck swung a pair of heavy boots whose laces were knotted together. He brought what must have been a waterproof tobacco-pouch out from a pocket, because when he had rolled a smoke he lighted the thing using a kind of Zippo (also from the pouch) and puffed upon it with an obvious relish.   (p. 155)

I have omitted the last sentence of the paragraph ('It was an astonishing spectacle') because it seems to me redundant, for the next sentence ('Hastening over to him I exclaimed: Christ

Almighty jimmy, where've you come from?') encapsulates the narrator's bewilderment. The surprise for the reader is perhaps the sudden appearance of an 'I', whose presence immediately makes the passage more subjective. In fact, the 'I's subsequent remark almost matches the strangeness of the spectacle itself – 'At least let me give you a pair of socks!' – though the epitome of incredulity is yet to come. In the last sentence the sea walker rejects the offer with a perplexing : 'No ... I'm not supposed to.'

What all these vignettes, owing to their inevitable constrictions, have in common is an invitation to the reader to puzzle and speculate, to make sense of the wealth of suggestions on offer, to look beneath the surface of things, and to question the trustworthiness of the narrative, especially if there is an 'I' whose view of things cannot be checked against another consciousness.

It is, of course, not the first time that we are confronted with a surreal situation in Kelman. Surreal elements are part of the baggage of Modernism, including Kelman's own brand of modernist realism. Think only of the eerie 'The Hon' or, in a different mode, the extraordinary thought-processes of the secluded speaker-narrator in 'Not not while the giro' or, again, the absurd contemplation of the possibility of a small bird crashing into another beach-walker ('The small bird and the young person' in *The Burn*). There is, then, thematic as well as atmospheric and narrative consistency in the short-story corpus. The industrial accident in 'A Rolling Machine', for example, is redolent of 'Acid', even though being told from a different perspective and in a differently inflected voice. Over 'Old Francis', which opens the volume, hangs a menace of imminent violence, as in 'The Witness', but with the difference that here the observer is not on the margins but becomes himself the target of the threats of a gang of youths. Then there are the numerous city walkers, pub-goers and punters, though again on more than one occasion there is a novel element, as in the hilarious miniature 'Cute Chick!', where 'this talkative old lady with a polite English accent' (*Greyhound*, p. 71) penetrates into the all-male world of the Glasgow betting shops to rake in a lot of money.

Still, it has been asked whether such marked consistency rather than notable development does not signal a failure. Douglas Gifford seems to assume a kind of stasis while immediately discounting it as a weakness: 'It's not a criticism that the stories in any of the three main collections . . . could fit in any of the others – and that almost any of the longer stories could supply a title for a consequently re-shuffled volume.'[2] Well, not all the titles possess the intriguing quality of 'Not not while the giro' or 'Greyhound for Breakfast'. But the main objection is surely that there is, in fact, significant thematic and character expansion in *Greyhound*. A substantial number of stories, from 'Renee' to 'Forgetting to mention Allende' to 'The Small Family' to 'A Sunday evening' to, indeed, 'Greyhound for Breakfast', treat gender and familial relations, even though the wife or partner may be offstage. Even assuming that some of the stories in *Greyhound* are of an older mark, waiting in a drawer to be looked at carefully and coldly from a remove, it is undeniable that the balance of loners and sociable or family men has altered. Also worth noting is that, contrary to *Not Not While the Giro* and *Lean Tales*, which recirculated some material from the small-press publications, only one out of the forty-seven stories is a reprint ('Fifty Pence' from *Three Glasgow Writers*).

The amount of work assembled in *Greyhound* makes towards greater scope and variety in almost every respect: length, subject matter, character, mood, emotion, use of register, tone of voice, narrative angle (for the first time there is a story told from the perspective of a woman, 'A Sunday evening'), even layout ('dear o dear', for example, is shaped like a concrete poem). So, while Kelman's range of abilities already shone up in the earlier collections, they are not only richly confirmed here but also put to the test with striking assurance.

Since the title story has been well served by commentators[3] I would like to discuss two others, which are paired through their sequential ordering in the book. Both are organized around a male character and his domestic problems. The wife or partner never makes an appearance except through the mind of the principal character, yet structurally she is present. Both stories start off as third-party narratives but quickly shift into free indirect discourse.

'not too long from now tonight will be that last time', an unmistakable Kelman title, belongs with the shorter pieces. It begins:

He was walking slowly. His pace quickened then slackened once more. He stopped by the doorway of a shop and lighted a cigarette. The floor was dry, a sort of parquetry. He lowered himself down to sit on his heels, his arms folded, elbows resting on his knees, his back to the glass door. (p. 47)

The change of pace and the halt reflect the unnamed character's state of indecision. He has been out in the night and can now neither bring himself to go home and creep into the marriage bed nor simply vanish. Although 'that would be great. He was not up to it. It was not something he felt capable of managing. It was not something he felt capable of' (p. 47). His present problem is the inability to face the woman and tell the truth, all aggravated by a natural taciturn disposition and, perhaps, inarticulacy: 'There were his silences. That inability he had to get out of himself' (p. 47). There are faint echoes of Hines here, though Hines would not have dreamed of leaving his wife and son. But in this case there is no mention of children.

The story is circular, it ends as it began, with the same change of pace: 'He inhaled on the cigarette then raised himself up and bent his knees a couple of times, before pacing on. After a time he slowed, but was soon walking more quickly' (p. 48). From this it can be concluded that 'tonight' no final decision will be reached, though maybe 'not too long from now'. But, if the title expresses the character's thought or hope rather than the narrator's commentary, the doubts concerning his capacity to clear off remain. It is one of the typically indecisive attempts at decision making that we come across so frequently in Kelman's fiction.

Stripped down to the barest essentials, the story dramatizes, if that is the right word, such a universal situation that it is easy to overlook how it is socially rooted. The man walks, he does not drive home. Squatting down is an age-old proletarian habit. The notion of 'taking a room perhaps with full board in some place far away' (p. 47), in other words repairing to a working-class hostel, would not have occurred to a well-off person.

'Forgetting to mention Allende', the other and much longer story, not only declares its class connotations from the start; it can also be located in time. The situation at the beginning superficially resembles that of *The Busconductor Hines*, only, instead of water, it is milk boiling and bubbling over, and the househusband who rushes to lift the pan off the cooker is alone with his little daughter. There is a wife ('Dont go telling mummy about the milk now eh' [*Greyhound*, p. 49]), but she is out, working 'as a cashier in a supermarket, nonstop the whole day' (p. 54), as we learn later. However, contrary to Hines, McGoldrick is not at home because he is a shiftworker, but because he is unemployed: 'He opened the newspaper at the sits. vac. col.' (p. 51). The other two children are in the primary school. The family must be newcomers in the housing scheme because McGoldrick is still painting and trying to get used to the noise level from the neighbouring flats: 'The walls were, like wafer fucking biscuits. Before flitting to the place he had heard it was a good scheme, the houses designed well, good thick walls and that, they could be having a party next door and you wouldnt know unless they came and invited you in. What a load of rubbish' (pp. 49–50). All these facts are established within two pages, and on their basis the narrative proceeds to give no more than a hint at the psychological and emotional state of a man coping with the evidently new role of a househusband. McGoldrick neither hates nor loves the domestic chores. Being housebound just bores him, but having to take the girl to the nursery or the boys to school makes matters worse. 'He always came out of the place feeling like an idiot' (p. 51). It is not clear whether he meets with taunts and raised eyebrows or whether he is just ashamed of this indirect public confession of the failure to find work. Unintentionally an old man who brings his grandchildren to the nursery stabs into the wound by scoffing at the unemployed:

> Between you and me Tommy there's a few staying about here that look as if a hard day's graft would kill them! Know what I mean? naw, I dont know how they do it; on the broo and that and they can still afford to go out get drunk. Telling you, if you took a walk into that pub down at the shopping centre you'd see half of them were drawing social security. Aye, and you couldnt embarrass them! (p. 52)

McGoldrick manages to keep quiet but when the old man makes as if to continue he takes to his heels.

Unobtrusively, the story establishes a man's difficulty of coming to terms with an unhabituated situation. Enforced idleness and public stigma may gnaw at McGoldrick's self-respect, but he never grudges his wife the job. It is true that he acutely registers her exhaustion after the long working day: 'She hardly had the energy for anything' (p. 54). But the text does not question the new gender relations. There is subdued anger in these pages but when it threatens to erupt it is directed against the well-dressed religious proselytes at the door, 'Mormons probably' (p. 54), who would like to shake him out of his atheism. Once again, McGoldrick controls himself. He does not start swearing until they have left: 'He had forgotten to mention Allende. He always meant to mention Allende to the bastards. Fuck it' (p. 55). It is a baffling 'global' connection, almost in the manner of a conceit of the 'Metaphysical' poets, but for McGoldrick the smugness of these missionaries is linked to the sinister manœuvres behind the violent coup against the Chilean President.

The unexpected reference to Allende at the end of the story and one to music records at the beginning help to situate the story in the mid-1970s. Since then the situation sketched here has become more widespread, more universal. All over Europe the twin forces of deindustrialization and privatization have destroyed hundreds of thousands of jobs, and in the process have devalued the skills of working-class males and diminished their traditional role as breadwinners. At the same time, fresh job opportunities in the retail and service sector have opened up for women. This in turn has led to a gradual erosion of gender roles, but the example of McGoldrick's wife's cashier job demonstrates that exploitation has not disappeared but is now being inflicted in even greater measure upon the women, to say nothing about the large segment of society today living under the poverty line.

Much more commonly broached by female writers with a working-class agenda, such as the early Pat Barker, Agnes Owens and Livi Michael, who examine these social changes from the perspective of the working women and mothers, 'Forgetting to mention Allende' inspects them from the position of an unemployed father capable of shedding his patriarchal skin.

There is sometimes a kind of *Wiedererkennungseffekt* in these stories. Look at this, the implied author seems to be intimating, you may have seen this before, but have you ever looked at it in this light, in such circumstances, among people like that? This 'recognition effect' can work in both realist and intertextual ways; realist in that readers, pulled in and involved in a story, can compare and contrast their own experiences with those on the page; intertextual in that they may see instructive parallels as well as differences between one (Kelman) story and another. In any case, the reception of *Greyhound* was so enthusiastic that the hardcover edition had to be reprinted the same year and that it became the first of Kelman's books to be marketed by a major New York publisher, Farrar, Strauss and Giroux in 1988.

In the twenty stories of *The Burn* (1991), eighteen of which appear in book form for the first time,[4] the emphasis on familial and social relations is given further weight. It is true that there are also stories of, or allusions to, break-ups, interestingly and in contrast to 'not too long from now tonight will be that last time' in some cases initiated by the women ('A decision' and 'Naval History'), in others not attributable to any one ('A walk in the park', 'From the window', 'Lassies are trained that way'). But failure of relationship is not the keynote of the collection, rather repeatedly a reaching-out to others, a not always successful attempt to make contact, an (often silent) cry for understanding and togetherness, for solace and comfort. What is more, the volume promotes fellow-feeling for the characters in these stories. This has not always been the case in Kelman's fiction. Compassion for Tammas, the chancer, or Doyle, the paranoid teacher, or the feverishly fantasizing narrator in 'Not not while the giro' does not come easily. By contrast, in *The Burn* it encompasses many of the central figures. It extends to both actors in the stories of parting couples and is certainly not withheld from the first-person narrator in 'Naval History' (where the break-up is more incidental).

The latter story has a deceptively autobiographical ring. A writer whose first name is James but whom his friends call 'Jimmy' and his family 'Jim' (the opposite in real life) bumps into two old friends as he is about to leave a bookshop. They are rather overwhelming, hugs and kisses and all, and insist on offering him a pile of books (on Hollywood stars and naval history, for example), in which he is not in the least interested. They seem to get some things wrong, remember him as a writer of 'wee stories with a working-class theme' (p. 95), whereas he considers himself a playwright, but they are suspiciously well informed about his private life, his divorce from Mary (Marie in real life, but still happily married). They also know all about his bus conductor's past, his slender means and his left-wing leanings ('a failed trades-union organiser, plus you're a failed socialist' [p. 95]), whereas Jimmy, the first-person narrator, defines his concerns as 'communistic', neither of which is exactly congruent with the position of the writer James Kelman.

The story becomes 'intriguing' in yet another sense, when the encounter mutates from forced jocularity into sinister nightmare as the two acquaintances of old reveal themselves to be plain-clothes police who eventually take him into custody. It is a Kafkaesque situation, in which Jimmy desperately attempts to stay sane in an increasingly hostile environment, which includes the bookshop manager. Yet the scene is not without its absurd side as he is all the time having to balance this unwieldy pile of unwanted books in his outstretched arms. But what comedy there is is a comedy of dark menace, taking place in a recognizably 'real' world, which makes it different from *In the Night*.

A masterpiece is the concluding story 'by the burn', which has lent its name to the collection. It consists of a six-page-long uninterrupted (i. e. unindented) narrative in which a man is on his way, as so often on foot, from a block of flats across a marshy waste ground to a railway station where he is to set out for a job interview. Every now and then he slips and sinks into the mud, on one occasion almost losing a shoe: 'Imagine if he had lost the fucking boot but Christ almighty, hirpling down the road for the train then into the interview office, trying to explain to the folk there how you had just lost your shoe in a fucking swamp' (p. 239). But his good spirits sink when a downpour starts and he cannot even see the stepping-stones on which he usually crosses the now swollen stream. He senses, and the reader with him, that he will never make it to the interview. He belongs with Kelman's losers, poor buggers who are always thrown off balance by some minor incident or obstacle, with the odds never staked in their favour. 'You just couldnt win, you just couldnt fucking win man never, you could never win' (p. 242). Why did he not take a car? Can't afford one. Why not a coat? The same story. 'He really did need a coat man this was just stupid. He had one right enough he just didnt wear the fucking thing, he didnt like it. It was too big for him for a start, it was his brother-in-law's. You could have wrapped it round him twice' (p. 241). Sometimes one can distinguish between the narrator and the inner voice, the thoughts of the man. But often the narrative changes so imperceptibly from one to the other that the two become indistinguishable, especially since both move in the same register and there are, as usual, no speech marks. This is, of course, part and parcel of Kelman's approach, to narrow the gap so as to avoid authorial (and, by implication, authoritarian) intrusion, or, in positive terms, to exhibit closeness to, and compassion with, the character: 'Fucking bogging mud man a swamp, an actual swamp, it was a fucking joke. He pulled his foot clear but the boot was still lodged there like it was quicksand and it was going to get sucked off and vanish down into it forever' (p. 239). This is the opening, and one could argue that the first sentence gives us the man's voice, the second the narrator's. And for a time one has the impression that the narrator limits himself to the description of the physical minutiae of the man's exposure to the forbidding nature and weather conditions, while leaving personal details (that the man is married with a daughter, leads a precarious life on an inaccessible council estate, is presently off for a job interview) to himself, the man's inner mind. This is what one might guess from the first passage quoted ('Imagine if he had lost'), but in the second ('He really did need a coat man') it becomes more difficult to identify the voice.[5]

If this were the whole story, a man stranded under a tree, where he has sought shelter, and thus missing an all-important job opportunity, it would still be moving, but not so special. However, the story takes a breathtaking turn, so unbearably painful for the character, and so deeply disturbing for the reader, that it becomes as unforgettable as 'Acid'. Shivering with cold under that tree the man suddenly feels as if somebody is watching him. Something half-spiritual, half-physical, an apparition, but also 'a tremor, a spasm' grips him:

> But it was his daughter, it was his daughter. Like her ghost was somewhere. He knew it. He knew what it was exactly. Because it was the sand pit. It was right across the burn from where he was standing and if it was winter and the leaves had fell you would see right across and the sandpit was there, it was right there, just on the other side. Aw dear, the wee fucking lassie. Aw dear man aw dear it was so fucking hard so fucking awful hard, awful hard so fucking

73

awful hard. Oh where was the wife. He needed his fucking wife. He needed her. He needed her close. He needed her so fucking close he felt so fucking Christ man the sandpit, where the wee lassie and her two wee pals had got killed. Hiding out playing chases. Aye being warned to steer clear but in they went and then it collapsed on them, and it trapped them, all these tons of earth and they had all got suffocated. Aw dear. Aw dear. (pp. 242–3)

After this it is difficult to read on. And I imagine that it must have been hard for Kelman, too, to write on. But the story does not end with the man's breakdown. We learn that, although the accident happened many years ago, he has, contrary to his wife, never been able to cope with the loss of his daughter. It is not the only time in this collection that men weep. Kelman's mastery consists in the seemingly effortless handling of the transition from one state of mind of the character to the other.

A similarly unexpected, though perhaps not quite as convincing twist occurs in the opening story, 'Pictures', where a man in a practically empty cinema cannot concentrate on what happens on the screen and watches instead furtively the other movie-goers in his row, an elderly woman and a younger one who is crying. Overcome by pity, but also driven by a desire to make contact – for he is clearly a loner – he offers to get her a coffee from the foyer. But his hopes for entering into a conversation or more are thwarted, so that he begins to speculate about the reasons for her distress and eventually pictures her – the other meaning of the title – as a prostitute in trouble. This in turn, but again quite shockingly for the reader, brings back to him memories of a day in his childhood on which he had prostituted himself 'for a pile of loose change' (p. 12), less than fifty pence, to a man in a public toilet: 'it was so bad it was like a horror story except it was real, a living hell' (p. 11).

Both in 'Pictures' and in 'by the burn' harrowing memories connected with childhood surface as if from the bottom of a burn, the stream of a past life, and float on the protagonist's mind. And in both cases the agitated male seeks solace from a female. These two stories do not frame the volume for nothing. In story after story (childhood) memories are stirred up. However, not all of them are as unpleasant or of central importance. In 'A walk in the park', 'A Memory', 'Naval History', 'From the Window' and 'the Christmas shopping' they are more tempered or lighthearted, and also more incidental, while in the ironically entitled 'Real Stories' they may not even be childhood recollections at all since the female figure invents 'wee stories about her girlhood with outcomes that were different from real life' (p. 157). Stephen Bernstein's observation that in *The Burn* 'everyone has a sad store of memories to sort through' and that 'everyone is a sufferer' thus needs to be qualified.[6]

Memories are important in this collection, but so is the desire to overcome a crippling loneliness, to build good-faith communication, to save collapsing relationships or strike up new ones. If the characters in these stories labour under difficulties and problems, haunting memories being one of them, they are yet trying to 'cope', a recurring expression, which sums up both the dilemma in which they are stuck and their attempt to hold on and not go under. In 'by the burn' the depressed father 'felt better' after his breakdown, even though it is for him 'a fucking racing certainty' (p. 244) that one day he will die of a heart attack in the same kind of utter loneliness to which he has just been exposed. Towards the end of 'A walk in the park' the male thinks that 'he couldnt bloody cope, that was the problem, he couldnt bloody cope, with life' but is reassured by his lover that 'things arent as bad as that' (p. 24). Despair is never far, and the moviegoer in 'Pictures' appears to succumb to it at the end, but not after having reached out in vain to a fellow-human being.

The Burn contains more hints of Kelman's politics than any previous volume of short stories. From the second item, 'A walk in the park', which has a reference to John MacLean, to the penultimate one, 'events in yer life', which mentions Che Guevara, another martyr and icon of revolutionary socialism, there are numerous allusions to figures on the left, to the state of Scotland and to the implementation of neoliberal policies in Britain and the Third World. Related to this is Kelman's ongoing concern 'with when and how an obsessive eye can become the natural way to see'.[7] One such obsession is that of being watched by the eye of the law ('Unlucky', 'the chase'). Some characters are directly confronted with the police ('That's were I'm at', 'Naval History'). Others condemn them as 'the forces of law and order for the rich and wealthy, the upper class' ('Lassies are trained that way' [p. 149]). It is an obsession that takes on a larger-than-life dimension in the later novels.

6

Under Surveillance, Resisting: *A Disaffection; How Late it Was, How Late* and *Translated Accounts*

What binds Kelman's later novels together is their strong anti-authoritarianism, and especially their interrogation of the working of state agencies and apparatuses. The author seems to require the longer fictional form for this kind of sustained investigation, for his short-story collection *The Good Times* (1998), published between these novels, does not contain comparable reflections on, or acts of defiance to, the ruling order. It is not that the ranters and railers against class iniquity or oppression are totally absent from its pages. The incessant talker in 'Oh my darling', for example, works himself up into a rage because the record label His Master's Voice carries for him class connotations, and a modern café in which he feels out of place has a bourgeois touch. But such occasional outbursts of anger on the part of a nervous fantasizer more preoccupied with other things come as an aside rather than a full-blown diatribe in its own right. (Another story with the occasional dig against the political system is 'Into the Rhythm'.)

Or take the piece 'pulped sandwiches', which is set on a building site of the kind that we find in Ken Loach's film *Riff-Raff* (1991): small, with possibly subcontracted labour, poor tools and a 'spying' gaffer. The speaker-narrator of this story, an ageing builder, bitterly reflects on the changed working conditions: 'In the old days ye would have swung the sledge and nobody the wiser when ye stopped for a smoke, there wasnay nobody could tell except maybe they might have listened for the chip chip. But not this goddam hammer. Once ye stopped working they knew, they heard that silence' (*Good Times*, p. 44). Yet his distrust of the ganger is of no consequence. The story ends on a subdued, even docile note when the narrator grudgingly accepts working overtime on a Friday evening, despite having a date with 'the missis'. By contrast, *Riff-Raff* works towards a dramatic finale. After the sacking of one builder, who complained about the unsafe working conditions on the site, and an industrial accident, which kills or maims another, the film ends with a revolutionary beacon reminiscent of Souvarine's, the Anarchist's, sabotage of the coalmine in Zola's *Germinal*. Two incensed construction workers set fire to the building even though it will mean the loss of their jobs.

Nothing could be further removed from Kelman's method of storytelling. His narratives rarely culminate in such a dramatic climax. Just as their opening plunges the reader into an ongoing scene or dialogue, as in the case of 'pulped sandwiches', so they end inconclusively, with no particular point reached, or so it seems. They do not rely on plot, incident or conflict. Instead of elaborate lifelines, they present glimpses or fragments of ordinary, mostly uneventful, certainly unspectacular lives. Yet, for all its resigned mood, 'pulped sandwiches' may be closer to the social reality of Thatcherite Britain in the 1980s and 1990s than the angry *actionnisme* that concludes *Riff-Raff*.

Of course, the difference is not so much one of political angles as of generic possibilities. Modern short fiction, from James Joyce and Sherwood Anderson onward, has largely dispensed with pivotal action and concentrates instead on episodes or discontinuous sequences of incidents. In the film medium the pressure to build scenes into a story, action, drama is immense. Even Ken Loach, known as he is for his sparse use of scripts, cannot escape the constrictions imposed by the genre. Representatives of the author-cinema such as Jean Marie Straub or Eric Rohmer, who attempted to ignore the rules of the game, opting instead for long dialogues or a narrative voice, paid the price of neglect. The difference between a short story like 'pulped sandwiches' and a film like *Riff-Raff* is that in the story we enter the showing, as it were, halfway through and the reel mysteriously stops well before the end. Such a fleeting glimpse of a life resists closures of any kind, including politically desirable ones.

In the novel *A Disaffection* (1989), the anti-authoritarianism rests on the shoulders of Patrick Doyle, a sickened teacher, a worrying intellectual, not on the 'fucking hopeless reactionariness' (p. 119) of his father, a factory worker, or his unemployed brother. Patrick's stance is established in four distinct, if closely related ways: his classroom behaviour, his view of the educational system, his attitude to his superiors and his heroes from the past.

The four classroom scenes in the novel are distributed over various age groups, from first year to sixth year. But some common features of Patrick's conduct emerge. First he treats the children as equals, as would-be adults:

Right then, one more: Animi egestas! Immediate translation! Ian!
Is it to do with poverty of the mind sir?
Yes sir, precisely. Now class, the lot of ye, repeat after me: Our parents, who are the poor, are suffering from an acute poverty of the mind.
The smiling faces.   (p. 24)

Underneath the obvious joke of returning the 'sir' to a first-year boy there is the respect for the pupils whom Patrick treats uncondescendingly, without in any way blinding himself to the different positions of teachers and kids. As might be expected, he is not only against the reintroduction of the belt, but also rejects the widespread notion that today's schoolchildren are being mollycoddled.

Secondly, Doyle sees in them individuals, not an amorphous group. He knows something about their family background and is not ashamed to connect it with his own:

Hey Raymond, what does your da do for a living?
He's on the broo just now Mister Doyle.
Aw aye. What has he worked at last?
Eh he worked in a factory....
Patrick nodded; he looked at the rest then back to Raymond: My da's been working in a factory for the past twenty-two year – that's when he's no having fucking heart attacks. He's a real yin so he is, a right fucking numbskull. He's got a wee baldy heid and sometimes I feel like giving it a brush with a brillo pad.
LOUD LAUGHING.   (p. 194)

In such an atmosphere of frankness and mutual respect the students have no hesitation in questioning him about the motives for his decision to leave the school. Does he not let them down? And Patrick winces at the suggestion.

Thirdly, while Patrick is exacting in his use of philosophical sources, he is clearly not bent on cramming knowledge into the children. As the narrator puts it: 'He was the kind of teacher who likes to spend an entire period on essential side issues' (p. 23). Argument comes before curriculum. His overarching aim is to give them a 'proper grounding in reality' (p. 182), that is, make them aware of their own situation in terms of class and gender, and sensitize them to power relations in society and official versions of the 'truth'.

Finally, Patrick's classes are informal, relaxed. Several times the narrative, like a drama text, gestures to laughter and smiles as responses of the learners. It is the ironical twist of his phrases that prevents the incantatory sentences, in the manner of the Lord's Prayer, from becoming an indoctrinating chorus:

> Repeat after me: We are being fenced in by the teachers
> We are being fenced in by the teachers
> at the behest of a dictatorship government
> at the behest of a dictatorship government
> in explicit simulation of our fucking parents the silly bastards
> in explicit simulation of our fucking parents the silly bastards
> Laughter. (p. 25)

But what is it that drives a caring and committed teacher of the mark of Patrick Doyle into resignation and depression? Why does he throw in the towel? The answer is that with one-half of his being he is a disciple (or, should one say, a prisoner) of Althusser (not named in the book) and as such recognizes the limited reach of his efforts to instil rational argument in the pupils. He leans towards the French philosopher's view of ideology as a structural distortion of perception fostered in us by the institutions through which we are socialized from infancy onward. One of those institutions is the school; in fact, ideology requires an apparatus such as the educational system and its practices in order to function, i.e. to represent 'not the system of the real relations which govern the existence of individuals, but the imaginary relation of those individuals to the real relations in which they live'.[1] That is to say, we experience the real world and our place in it not directly and clearly, but obscured through the workings of ideology, which envelops social contradictions in a haze and interprets injustices in the interests of the dominant class. Thus the teacher recruited by the state to serve the educational apparatus becomes a cog in the wheel. All the critical energy Patrick can muster, all the counter-interpretations aiming to retrieve progressive impulses from reactionary canonical works of literature and philosophy, cannot detract from his complicity in keeping the lower classes subordinate. When all is said and done, he argues, you still perform 'the fencing-in job for a society you purport to detest right to the very depth of your being' (p. 87). Following from this grim analysis, the position of a radical schoolteacher becomes morally untenable. Patrick in conversation with an uncomprehending colleague: '[The] weans' heids get totally swollen with all that rightwing keech we've got to stuff into them so's we can sit back with the big wagepackets. It's us that keep the things from falling apart. It's us. Who else! We're responsible for it, the present polity' (p. 149). It is this unresolvable conflict between commitment and betrayal, plus his crippling loneliness, which drives Doyle to the verge of breakdown. Perhaps in a country like Scotland, with its revered tradition of learning for all, the proposition that, not just an individual dominie may be at fault, but the ethos of a whole profession is particularly devastating.

Patrick's tense relations with his superiors are the least of his problems, but they add another facet to his general hostility to the powers that be. His dubbing of the Deputy Head, MI6, says it all. The feeling of being under constant observation, whether real or projected, is part of his paranoid state of mind, an obsession he shares with countless other characters in Kelman's universe (see the above-mentioned building worker):

> A head could be seen passing along the corridor: and slowly, going slowly, as though in an attempt to overhear the slightest piece of untowardity. Patrick indicated the head and the class turned to see it. Notice that head! he called. You're probably all thinking it's a spy from Mister Big's office. And fucking right ye are cause that's exactly the case, the way of things, how matters are standing, at the present, the extant moment. Arse.   (p. 195)

Patrick's blood also boils when he thinks of Old Milne, the Headmaster. He ignores an appointment with him, partly to show his disrespect, partly to avoid questions about his rumoured political views. In fact, when the interview eventually takes place, all Patrick learns is that his transfer to another school has gone through. The ensuing altercations leave the reader wondering whether Patrick actually applied for the transfer, which he claims he cannot remember, or whether it is all a manœuvre to get rid of him. Whatever the truth, the outcome strengthens Patrick's feeling that he is up against impalpable powers, and contributes to his decision to chuck the job altogether. He simply fails to turn up for the afternoon classes.

A Disaffection abounds with what critics, following Julia Kristeva, have called 'intertextual' references, a suspect term because it suggests movement from text to text without human agency. Some names crop up particularly frequently: Goya, Goethe, Hölderlin, Hegel (sometimes by implication when there is talk of dialectics) and the Pythagoreans. A mixed bag no doubt, but the significance of the first four of Patrick's heroes should not be lost. Without exception they are contemporaries of the French Revolution. Mainlanders all of them, they were inevitably confronted with the turmoil of their times. Hölderlin and Hegel, born in 1770, belong to what one might call the generation of '89 – that is to say, they came of age in the 'dawn' in which it was 'bliss' to be alive (Wordsworth, also born in 1770, gets only one or two mentions, for reasons that will become clear in a moment). The upheaval they witnessed – Goya from very close quarters – appeared to herald the end of tyrannical rule and to hold the promise of universal liberation. Goethe had famously pronounced the beginning of a new era in the world's history after witnessing the cannonade of Valmy in 1792,[2] though he remained ambivalent about the French Revolution. Hegel believed the *Weltgeist* to have paraded on horseback in the person of Napoleon (born 1769). But, with the excesses of the revolutionary terror, the endless wars and finally the triumph of reaction throughout Europe, 'the good times', far from being imminent, receded ever further into the distance. How to cling to the old ideals, whether and how to become reconciled with reality, was the question now agitating the disappointed liberal and revolutionary artists, writers and philosophers.

Kelman, born 1946 (though not Doyle, who is just under 30 in a novel presumably set in the mid-1980s), is a child of 1968. You did not have to attend university to be roused by the war in Vietnam, the invasion of Prague, the cultural upsurge of the Sixties and the student revolts in Europe culminating in May 1968. Once again, great promises, hopes, dreams, ideals, projects of liberation were in the air. But after the excitement, the high-flown rhetoric, the carnival, the sobering was not long in coming. In Britain it arrived in the figure of Margaret Thatcher, and the year in which she first assumed office (1979) also spelt the end, for the time being, of Scotland's dream of independence. Except for the revolution in sexual mores, all the great libertarian visions, all the projects of socialist transformation, came to be buried or disavowed. One can see the appeal of Althusser's disenchanted thesis to the politically disappointed generation of '68. Here, too, therefore the spectacle of confusion and resignation, of radicals making their peace with the world, some succumbing to cynicism, others, like Doyle, wavering between conviction and despair.

There are, then, also psycho-social reasons for Doyle's absorption in the generation of '89. He is haunted by Goya's 'black period' because its vision of horror corresponds with his own 'black' mood. Images of 'revolution and disease and starvation and torture and murder and rape' (p. 118) crowd his mind. No wonder that during his recurring bouts of depression he is, like Hölderlin, approaching the point of crack-up. Again, like Hölderlin or young Werther, who is infatuated with a betrothed, he is in love with a married woman; and, like the great Romantic hero, he contemplates suicide. Just as Werther's obsession, encapsulated in Goethe's phrase 'Krankheit zum Tode' (malady towards death),[3] is more than an individual neurosis, but symbolizes a struggle against the oppressions of his contemporary life and the impossibility of obtaining freedom, so Patrick's psyche is the site of wider social and political conflicts.

Patrick considers himself a 'fucking no-user' (p. 199) because his teaching is not validated by his own political praxis. Contrary to some theoreticians he does not resort to the trick of selling his teaching as a political act. His decision to quit results from this frustration. So does the resolution: 'Facta non verba, from now on' (p. 186). And he challenges the pupils to do the same: 'Why dont yous go and blow up the DHSS office?' (p.

186). At the end of the novel, Patrick, walking the streets in a state of drunken stupor, pictures to himself smashing in the windows of every bank, building society and insurance company – 'anything at all connected with the financial institutions of the Greatbritish Rulers' (p. 335). Whether he will actually do it is another matter, just as it is uncertain whether the policemen on the other side of the road, who 'had appeared at the very thought of insurrection' (p. 336), want to arrest him. *A Disaffection* leaves, like so many of Kelman's works, nothing resolved.

But the appearance of the police is a reminder of that other, repressive state apparatus, whose function it is not to secure consensus for the maintenance of power, but to exercise control, if need be by violence. The novel is interspersed with references to the 'polis'. Two are posted outside the school and the hint that Doyle 'went to uni and became a member of the polis' (p. 139) serves as a reminder that policing the masses and forging consent are two sides of the same coin.

If *A Disaffection* ends with *surveiller*, *How Late it Was, How Late* (1994) begins with *punir*.[4] After having kipped in the open, the protagonist awakens, mysteriously with somebody else's shoes on, finds himself cornered by two plain-clothes police ('sodjers') and, after a brawl, ends in a police cell, with a broken rib and his eyesight gone. As Ian A. Bell has noted in an early commentary, the opening of the novel is a substantial rewriting of Kafka's tale 'Die Verwandlung' ('Metamorphosis'),[5] stripped of anything redolent of metaphysics. Instead the novel is grounded, in typically Kelmanesque fashion, in reality, the stark reality of the rough working class (as distinct from Kafka's equally ordinary, but middle-class existences). Sammy Samuels – the name recalls Kafka's Gregor Samsa and Milton's blind Samson Agonistes held prisoner by the Philistines – has not been transformed into an insect of sorts, but his life has undergone a no less dramatic change. Sammy's hell is not a dream or nightmare, but a 'daymare' (the expression is from *A Disaffection*, p. 120). Eyeless in Glasgow, without a penny in his pocket, he gropes his way from the police station to his girlfriend's home, only to find it deserted. The body and its physiological functions, always important in Kelman, assume a tactile primacy, as he learns painfully – in more senses than one – to readjust to his new situation. Given his ordeal, Sammy surprisingly rarely succumbs to self-pity or sentimentality. But then he has never been spoilt by life. A semi-skilled construction worker, he has jobbed on building sites when jobs were going and been involved in crime when there were none. On two separate occasions he landed in prison, which he accepted in a stoic mood: 'Ye do yer crime ye take yer time' (*How Late*, p. 15). For years surviving has been his only full-time occupation. So in characteristically resilient manner he sets about devising his 'wee survival plan' (p. 65):

> What can ye do but. Except start again so he started again. That was what he did he started again. It's a game but so it is man life, fucking life I'm talking about, that's all ye can do man start again, turn ower a new leaf, a fresh start, another yin, ye just plough on, ye plough on, ye just fucking plough on, that's what ye do, that was what Sammy did, what else was there I mean fuck all, know what I'm saying, fuck all. (p. 37)

If anything, this understates his astonishing feat of endurance. One source of strength is his irrepressible sense of ironic humour. Here he is propping himself against a wall for a rest during his groping journey home: 'He was gony stay there. So what if they tried to fucking lift him I mean what could they fucking charge him with? loitering with intent? A fucking good yin that, loitering with intent – intent to bump into a lamppost; bastards' (p. 44). However, this parody of the discourse of legal authority cannot relieve the bitter insight that this is a society where mishaps are blamed on the victims rather than on the perpetrators:

> [H]is hand got a hold on the left side door; he stepped down, down onto the road; onto the road, he had to find the kerb fast, fast man come on, come on. One time there was this guy stepped off the pavement, Argyle Street on a Saturday afternoon for christ sake crowds everywhere and there was a bus coming fast on the inside lane and the fucking wing mirror fucking blootered him man right on the fucking skull, blood belching out; what a crack! the driver jumping out the cabin and wanting to help the guy but the poor bastard got off his mark immediately, probably thinking he had done something wrong man damaged company fucking property or something and the driver was trying to get his name, so he got off his mark, staggering into this sprint – Sammy could see him yet, poor bastard, fucking blood everywhere. (pp. 85–6)

Just as Sammy is about to get his wits back, he is arrested again and subjected to endless interrogation. But why single out a small crook for such special treatment? It takes Sammy and the reader some time to put two and two together. During the pub crawl, which preceded his being beaten up and losing his eyesight in consequence, Sammy has been unfortunate enough to bump into a mate wanted by the police for some unspecified subversive activity. (As in Kafka, the absence of any definite charge only adds to the pervasive threatening atmosphere.) The mysterious Charlie Barr, a former shop steward, a political animal, perhaps a bomb-thrower, never turns up in the novel. But, through this contact, Sammy has now himself become a suspect 'political' case, *puni et surveillé*, which explains the arrival of the Special Branch on the scene.

However, the police is only one of the implacable forces that Sammy, in his lone survival struggle, is up against. Once he starts seeking compensation or only reregistration, so as not to lose Community Gratuities, he gets caught in the bureaucratic machinery of other authorities. The questioning by the doctor is not accompanied by manhandling, the threats may be more veiled (benefit cuts), the insensitive formalistic procedures and protocols of a Kafkaesque bureaucracy are carried on in public rather than behind closed doors, but the intended effect of these methods is the same as that dished out by the police: the claimant is to be intimidated and discouraged, in short disciplined. For Sammy, in this monstrously unequal battle with the tentacles of the (to him) invisible state kraken, it is all one. Does the doctor, he wonders, who lectures rather than examines him, collude with the police? On whose side is the exceedingly well-informed rep who offers to push his claim for compensation? The reader is made to share these uncertainties and anxieties through the narrative stance, which is completely restricted to the perceptions and rambling mindwork of a suddenly stone-blind man. His blackout regarding the details of his disastrous drinking tour makes for a patchy and fragmented picture.

One thing alone is certain, Sammy can trust nobody as he makes his stand against the police, medical and social security authorities. Even his drinking pals cut him, since word has been passed that politics is involved. It is not until the end that support comes movingly, if improbably, in the person of his 15-

year-old son from his broken-up family. Familial relations, rare in Kelman's early fiction, *The Busconductor Hines* excepted, become a point of hope and succour in the later works, especially the short stories.

The implicit intertextual hints to Kafka's works have already been mentioned. The equivalent of the explicit intertextual references in *A Disaffection* are the lyrics from folk and country music that litter the novel. Just as Patrick Doyle's mind was brimming with philosophers, artists, writers and their characters (including Kafka's Gregor Samsa and Joseph K.), so Sammy's consciousness is alive to fragments of song lyrics. And, just as Patrick's preoccupation with specific masters of the past was telling, so Sammy's choice of song-writers is revealing: Bob Dylan, Kris Kristofferson, Woodie Guthrie and Willie Nelson. Diverse as they are, their tunes and lyrics not only reflect Sammy's mood at various stages, but between them provide, much like the capacity for irony in adverse circumstances, a kind of spiritual prop, from which he can pick up new strength. For Sammy 'country music was for adults' (p. 156), and he especially relates to the 'outlaw stuff' (p. 155).

Several of the footloose characters who people the *Lean Tales* have a similar musical predilection. The speaker-narrator from 'the same is here again', who is roughing it in London, confesses, after he has broken into a car and found a Johnny Cash cassette: 'My life is haunted by country & western music' (*Lean Tales*, p. 13).[6] This nameless figure bears a close resemblance to Sammy, in his down-and-out state, his loneliness, his concern for his body and his Glaswegian background. 'the same is here again' may well have been a preliminary sketch for *How Late*.

Music is a need for Sammy, reading is, or was (will he have to learn Braille, he reflects), a pastime. True to his anti-prejudiced viewpoint, Kelman has made him quite naturally into a reader of books, although, Jack London's *John Barleycorn* apart, it is the contents of works rather than authors or titles that he remembers.

The end of *A Disaffection* saw the teacher running, in an imagined or real flight, from the police. *How Late* also ends with the protagonist on the run, dodging his surveillance with the help of two teenagers. 'Resisting Arrest', Cairns Craig entitled an essay on Kelman even before the publication of *How Late*.[7] Already Hines and Tammas, the protagonists of the two earlier novels, were running up against the authorities, inspectors and 'polis'. But in the later fiction the resistance of isolated and terrorized individuals against the sinister and repressive forces of the state has become more desperate, more articulate (Doyle) and more ingenious (Sammy).

Nowhere are state agencies more strongly identified as ruthlessly brutal instruments of terror than in *Translated Accounts* (2001), at once Kelman's most political and least tractable novel, if indeed 'novel' is an adequate term for a discontinuous narrative composed of anonymous eye/'I' witness accounts of life under military rule in an unspecified 'terrortory' (p. 149).[8] This country has a coastline and mountains, vendors of water and pumpkins. Some of its inhabitants drink wine, too. It might be Turkey, the Balkans in the 1990s, or Palestine in the 2000s; for geographical and political reasons – foreign observers *are* admitted – it cannot be Chechenia. The point is that it could be anywhere on the edge of the rich white world.

'There were bodies strewn throughout the building' (p. 1). The first sentence sets the tone for much of what is to come. Chilling references to bodies, precariously alive, mutilated or dead, accompany the reader to the very end: 'The body now lying still. A carcass, corpse, yes' (p. 313). Destinies of anonymous people are reported in a faltering spoken English: stories or hints of intimidation, expulsion, separation of family members, internment, rape, torture, disappearance, atrocities ('babyonets' [p. 40]), executions. But we equally hear of little survival strategies including desperate confessions of love and tenderness under impossible circumstances, and various acts of subterfuge and resistance against what are dubbed 'the authoritys' and 'the securitys'. The most memorable of these feats of resistance is embedded in one of the few accounts that is actually a story, 'a pumpkin story' (chapter 14), in which a pumpkin, or watermelon (the accounts differ), is thrown at a military official, splashing all over his 'insignia breast' (p. 124), for which the perpetrator immediately receives several bullets in his head. Occasional mentions of emails and the Internet, of visa cards and 'corporate worldwide banking and finance opera-tions' (p. 172), make it clear that we are in the present.

Pointers to state-inspired terrorist operations are not new in Kelman's work. Patrick Doyle reminded his fourth-formers that 'yous know there are people the same age as yourselves getting beaten up and tortured and killed in countries not all that far from here and I wont name them because if ye don't know what I'm talking about ye don't deserve to. People of twelve, thirteen, fourteen; they're getting tortured and murdered' (*A Disaffection*, p. 199). And this hinted, among others, at Ulster, where the British Government was found guilty of torture and inhuman treatment by the European Convention on Human Rights. In an interview from the same year Kelman spoke of 'US terrorism in Central and South America, Asia, Africa, the Middle East' and of the refusal of 'liberal media people' 'to see things – to bear witness'.[9]

Displacing the action from a recognizable urban Scotland to an unknown distant region not only directs our attention to the naked repression existing in other corners of the globe; it also establishes a relation of guilt between the metropolitan centres and the peripheral zones through either connivance with the local regimes or lack of solidarity with the victims. The link is provided by the frequent references to 'specialty individuals and professional expert people, lawyers, doctors, all professors and higher authoritys' (*Translated Accounts*, p. 80) visiting the country to investigate allegations of torture and summary executions. Kelman, steeped in the anti-expert Scottish common-sense philosophy, has only scorn for their mystifications and hair-splitting arguments, and for the advice these visitors have in store for people engaged in a struggle for life and death:

> At larger meetings in foreign countries our colleagues listened to conversations and leading statements . . . if this one or that one who is of fascist calling is also moral or has scruples derived from religious or ethical code, if a security is a 'kind security', or state official is just and fine a person in his own house, saying fine anecdotes to people, if torturers make jokes, these are witty people sensitive people, we must understand them.
>
> Colleagues entered into such discussion if one fascist was 'caring fascist', one racist was 'caring racist', what one torturer may be, one rapist, murderer of children, yes, murderer of children is 'caring murderer of children'. And if our colleagues said to them, But we know what securitys are, what are military operatives, what politicians of national government, lawyers, doctors, judiciary . . .

They said to us, No you must listen. 'Official politics' is 'you must listen politics', constitutional activity operating by rules and regulating principles embedded into stone by all gods and infallible creatures. (p. 170)

In the novel 'colleagues' seems to have replaced the either cautiously withheld, no longer valued or (by the translator) deliberately suppressed 'comrades'. An even more scathing criticism of the role of the foreign experts, and about the only instance of a bitter humour in these accounts, comes across in the 'lecture, re sensitive periods' (chapter 10). Here the usual scrambled transcription is compounded by a legalese from an international lawyer, who has urged on the locals the case of a schoolgirl attacked in his own country by a vicious dog, with a view to instruct his hearers that stories of atrocities and murders must be taken with caution and scrupulously verified before a verdict can be given:

And now of the child-victim, speak of her, this paragon child, puberty child in adolescence why she is walking home from school down this street and not another. What is her background. She is a child, she is female. She is reliable. Many girls do not distinguish easily as between fact, fiction. We know children, we were all children. Boys also, they invent fictions. Adults, yes, they too, it is a failing of all humans, tall tales. Mature responsible human adult citizens, who may have regard for stories, greater regard.

And for some children it is true, authoritys advise us, that they have been naughty in the district and this dog-owning fellow, as one responsible and law-abiding citizen, will try to correct all anti-societal behaviour of these younger hooligan elements. He takes this societal burden upon his own shoulders, peacekeeper and moral strategist, what you may, asking no recompense. And what rewards. Calumny. It is not only children seeking revenge and of whom this girlish paragon is almost certainly one, or has friends she aids in such revenge, acting on their behalf.

And at Hospital Casualty department, upon examination of this victim female paragon, did one so-called doctor or doctors verify existence of so-called bite, that teeth were responsible, that dogs were responsible, time of occurrence of bite, this teeth-wound, might it not have been older . . .

Is his knowledge specialised knowledge. Perhaps he cannot distinguish dog bites one from another. Does teeth-wound indicate a dog in particular or could it be the teeth-wound of any dog found on planet Earth, dachshund to Rottweiler. Can first doctor distinguish between teeth of a dog and each other species of animal known to mankind. May not there be one unknown animal in lost jungles south of Borneo whose teeth markings are similar. Was one or more unusual animals discovered in vicinity of girl's village that day. (pp. 82–3)

This is the familiar Kelman, branding in a Swiftian rage the absurd casuistry of the legal profession. But *Translated Accounts* defamiliarizes even readers who have grown accustomed to Kelman's Glaswegian speaker-narrators through a language literally tortured and strangled and disembodied, for there is no way that we can identify or empathize with the nameless individuals behind these collated abstracts of interviews and statements. And yet, like one of his witnesses, Kelman is only too aware that 'the name of an individual is important' (p. 314). Making them anonymous is to heighten the pervasive atmosphere of fear, confusion, distrust and uncertainty that envelops these 'imperfect speakers'. Although the emotions and anxieties vented in their testimonies allow for some differentiation, the homogenized diction in which these are rendered effaces the fractured individual consciousnesses that struggle for articulation. As the fictitious preface warns us, this may be the work of translators or transcribers who are not native English speakers, but it may also be due to modifications made 'by someone of a more senior office' (p. ix).

In his Chomsky essay discussed above, Kelman alludes to a gulf in understanding between the comfortably situated reader or spectator, whose senses may have been dulled by statistics, and the harassed victim of organized violence: 'Reports by refugees of atrocities are difficult to cope with. We are not used to such testimony, not unless, perhaps, the refugees are in flight from the same ideological enemy as ourselves' (*Judges*, p. 146). *Translated Accounts* illustrates this point through the foregrounding of language. The terrifying strangeness of the experiences reported here, hardly 'translatable' into the mother tongue, highlights the enormous difficulty of connecting with other people's pain. This is not so much a matter of the inadequacy of the translations as of the different positions of speakers and listeners. In the face of proliferating disasters and war zones, reported daily, in fact hourly on such channels as CNN, from across the globe, we may have reached a point of 'compassion fatigue', as the *Times Literary Supplement* reviewer put it.[10] By telling us their troubles in what has become a global language, interviewees address us directly, yet cannot count on understanding, far less help or solidarity. Kelman's novel must be one of the first to confront the political and linguistic implications of the rise of English as a *lingua franca*, itself founded on political and economic domination, and its uses in the non-print media. The questions that *Translated Accounts* raises can be formulated in general terms: under which circumstances are such utterances, statements, interviews, interrogations collected? Who transmits them to whom, with what intention and to which effect? In gesturing towards these questions, Kelman alerts us, once again, to the political uses made of language by those wielding power, and especially those in control of the communication channels.

With this uncompromisingly experimental novel Kelman has come a step closer to his declared aim of stripping the narrative of any remnants of elitist subjectivity. There is certainly nothing left here resembling a conventional 'third-party narrative voice'. But he has done so at the cost of representation and readability, to whose limits we are pushed. While persistent sympathetic readers will eventually get used to the broken rhythmic pattern generated by the method employed, much in the way that they first had to adapt to, but then became familiarized with, the insistent Glasgow accent, it is unlikely that they will respond to a non-localized setting, non-identifiable voices and their linguistic amalgam. As a highly self-conscious writer Kelman was obviously prepared to take the risk of radically undercutting readers' expectations. Whether the formidable formal rigour applied to *Translated Accounts* will not lead to a 'compassion fatigue' of readers remains to be seen.

7

Postscript: *You Have to be Careful in the Land of the Free*

Kelman's sixth novel retains the extra-European setting of *Translated Accounts*, but reverts to a Glaswegian voice. As the title indicates, *You Have to be Careful in the Land of the Free* (2004) is set in the United States, picturing a 'Skarrish' expatriate on the eve of a visit 'hame'. However, what is new in this voice is not only the mock American inflection – resulting from its owner's twelve-year stay in the country – but its narrative monopoly. There is now only the consciousness of the protagonist, the perspective of 'a non-assimilatit alien' on the margins of American society.

But poverty of condition in Kelman never means poverty of the mind. Already on the first page the narrator tells us that he could have read a book in the motel near the airport instead of opting for the night out. And later he confesses that while he made a meagre living from dead-end jobs in restaurants, bars, galleries and a security agency, his real ambition had been to write a political crime novel centred on a hero who 'wasnay the usual apolitical right-wing hollywood prick, his sympathies went to the underdog, he was anti-cops and anti-robbers, anti-authoritarian, he was also a good anarchist; anti-sexist, anti-homophobic, anti-racist, pro-justice, pro-truth, pro-asylum seeker, pro-immigration, pro-equality' (p. 67). Alas, the 'private-eye ditty' never materialized. Like other things in Jeremiah Brown's life, it is a story of failure: 'I wasnay able to get on with it' (p. 67). The reasons are unclear, but Kelman, never afraid of exposing a character's flaws, intimates here that political correctness in itself does not achieve much.

Within a couple of pages the novel stakes out a terrain familiar to Kelman readers. When the narrator describes himself – almost parodying a recurring type of character-drawing – as a 'compulsive, obsessive, addictive personality, the usual' (p. 2) we know what we are in for. From the drinking and (in the past also) smoking and gambling habits, to the whining, suicide-contemplating, railing and fantasizing moods, all the traits that we have come to associate with the author's male loners are there. Except that Jeremiah had for a time abandoned his solitary life by entering an extra-marital relationship and trying to become a 'faimly man', and his by turns tender, sentimental and self-reproachful memories of his 'ex' and the little daughter form one major strand of the novel. Here is one of the rare moments of bliss in a Kelman fiction:

> When I was out with her, I would forget what I was doing, what I was thinking, and just be mentally lost just suddenly there in the heat of the moment and standing there or else walking and just like whatever, talking the gether – ye could have felt like kissing the pavement ye were so glad to be alive and just doing that, what ye were doing, going along the street having a conversation, it was amazing, and putting yer arm round her. (pp. 116–17)

The relationship with Yasmin, a jazz singer, is at once the high point of Jeremiah's American years and, when it breaks down, 'one of the mair traumatic experiences'. No wonder his thoughts always circle back to her as the night draws on, and the drinks go down, and he reviews his life in 'Uhmerka'. Reminiscences and musings alternate with preoccupations and recriminations in what is one long interior monologue, occasionally interrupted by some observations and exchanges in the bar, but for the reader unrelieved by chapter breaks or spaces on the page.

Relief comes through the humorous asides, the best of which have a political edge, as when in one of his bleaker moods the protagonist reflects that instead of trying to write a thriller he should have taken out a patent for some decent toilet paper:

> In twelve years in this country I had had many a good shite but never a good fucking wipe man they didnay know how to make toilet paper. Imagine that! supreme destroyer of the planet; leader in world exploitation, in the destruction of all human endeavour; supporter of the tyrant and genocidal murderer, yet they couldnay wipe their dowp without sticking a finger through the paper, dear

93

oh dear. Unless it was intentional. That hadnay occurred to me. It was a dastardly plot! (pp. 74–5)

Slipping from the physical to the political to the paranoid is a Kelman specialty. But what is the mild paranoia of an individual against the organized hysteria of a state, the novel seems to be asking. It abounds with references to the 'alienigenae', immigrants, 'furnirs', Red Card Class III holders like Jeremiah (never far from deportation) and the Patriot Holding Centers in which suspects are kept. Without ever naming September 11, though occasionally alluding to the 'continuing war against evil', Kelman recreates the climate of horror, fear and suspicion that has arisen and is being exploited for devious ends. A more macabre aspect of this publicly fomented atmosphere is a ploy known as the 'persian bet' (contracted from 'perishing'), whereby desperate bankrupts fly a carrier known to have a pitiable safety record while their dependents see a bookie who offers odds on air-crash probability. 'Flight became a moral and social obligation for down-the-line male fellers. For traveling gamblers it was a dream come true. Either way ye were a winner. If ye survived ye lost the bet but if ye perished yer faimly collected the cash' (p. 98).

Jeremiah learns about this racket from his gambling partners, but he is directly confronted with the security paranoia when as a father-to-be he applies, somewhat improbably, for a job in an airport security agency and, is, despite his declared 'libertarian socialist atheist' position, taken on. Politics, like religion, had been a taboo subject in his relationship, ruled out by Yasmin. For Jeremiah, always ready to burst out into a 'polemical diatribe against the evils of imperialism, colonialism, capitalism and all the rest of it' (p. 437), this must have been a trial, so that, paradoxically, as something not spoken about the subject had weighed on their relationship. 'What is wrong with my country you go to such lengths of ironic savagery?' (p. 180) one of his security colleagues asks Jeremiah. He doesn't answer, but the reader, privileged with insights into his mind, knows exactly what is wrong, and that it isn't 'this great country of yours', but something about its *polis* and policies coupled with powerfully entrenched economic interests that is to blame. It is to the promise of a 'Land of the Free', its popular and submerged sections and their radical tradition that the novel's sympathies are directed, just as it is dedicated to 'my family in USA, those I know and those I don't know, and also for my friends there'.

But to read the novel as targeting solely the political climate of one country in the throes of security paranoia would be to take a narrow view. Institutionalized racism and class warfare from above can be found in many places. And for all his idiosyncrasies, Jeremiah's frustration and alienation are lived, as individually experienced social maladies, by countless poor immigrants worldwide, many of them in much worse circumstances than 'an inkliz-talking pink guy' (p. 260) in North America.

The narrator is not such a memorable figure as the bus conductor Hines, the disaffected teacher Doyle or blind Sammy Samuels, but he is, literally, their distant relative, and he comes closest to them at the end when he is on the move, in the street. With head and bladder full of beer, he is searching for a toilet and somehow gets lost in a snowdrift in this unlit mid-western township until he is finally, and menacingly, confronted by a cop. This conclusion bears a strong resemblance to *A Disaffection*, only that instead of hurling bricks at the windows of financial institutions Jeremiah throws snowballs after a rottweiler and its owner ('Frankenstein') and at a house whose occupiers had not answered his call for help, pathetically missing them all.

Notes

CHAPTER 1. INTRODUCTION

1. Ian A. Bell, 'James Kelman', *New Welsh Review*, 10 (1990), 18.
2. Richard Cobb quoted in Alan Taylor, 'Some Humour Down in Hell', *Observer Scotland*, 22 October 1989; cf. also Cobb's statement in 'Books of the Year', *Spectator*, 22 December 1984.
3. Julia Neuberger quoted in *The Times*, 12 October 1994; headline in *Independent*, 12 October 1994; Simon Jenkins in *The Times*, 15 October 1994; Ron McKay in *Scotland on Sunday*, quoted in Neal Ascherson, 'Will Kelman's London Cheers Pave the Way for Glasgow Sneers?', *Independent on Sunday*, 16 October 1994. Geoff Gilbert reviews some more shocked responses in his article 'Can Fiction Swear? James Kelman and the Booker Prize', in Rod Mengham (ed.), *An Introduction to Contemporary Fiction* (Cambridge, 1999), 230–1.
4. 'Dillons bookshops cut the £14.99 by 25 per cent hoping to inspire sale. Waterstone in Hampstead, traditional home of the well-read, did not sell a copy', *The Times*, 13 October 1994. Richard Todd reckons that *How Late it Was, How Late* sold only about a quarter of the usual 1980s/1990s prize-winner copies. See his *Consuming Fictions: The Booker Prize and Fiction in Britain Today* (London, 1996), 101.
5. Kirsty McNeill, 'Interview with James Kelman', *Chapman*, 57 (1989), 4.
6. Quoted by Robert Scholes, whose 1967 edition of *Dubliners* (London) restored the dashes that Joyce preferred to indicate dialogue; see his 'Note on the Text', 259.
7. H. Gustav Klaus, 'Kelman for Beginners', *Journal of the Short Story in English*, 22 (1994), 130.
8. Angus Calder, *Revolving Culture: Notes from the Scottish Republic* (London, 1994), 2.
9. As the Bibliography shows, literary linguists have had a field day with Kelman's works. Interestingly, academics appear no less

mesmerized by the Booker Prize than the general public, for how can one explain the explosion of Kelman studies after 1994?
10. McNeill, 'Interview', 5.
11. Bertolt Brecht, 'Weite und Vielfalt der realistischen Schreibweise', *Gesammelte Werke*, vol. 19 (Frankfurt, 1967), 340 (my translation – HGK).
12. Heinrich Böll, 'Frankfurter Vorlesungen', in *Werke: Kölner Ausgabe*, vol. xiv: *1963–1965*, ed. Jochen Schubert (Cologne, 2002), 144 (my translation – HGK).
13. Quoted by Ian Black, 'Kelman Lines up his Next Shot', *Sunday Times Scotland*, 16 October 1994. Ngugi's *Decolonising the Mind: The Politics of Language in African Literature* was published in 1986.

CHAPTER 2. FOOTLOOSE IN COUNTRY AND CITY

1. Douglas Gifford, 'Discovering Lost Voices', *Books in Scotland*, 38 (1991), 4.
2. Alasdair Gray on the dust jacket of Kelman's collection *Greyhound for Breakfast* (1987).
3. Caroline Macafee, 'Glasgow Dialect in Literature', *Scottish Language*, 1 (1982), 50.
4. Duncan McLean, 'James Kelman Interviewed', *Edinburgh Review*, 71 (1985), 67.
5. Ibid. 77.
6. Hamilton collected his stories from *Three Glasgow Writers* plus a few new ones in the volume *Gallus, Did You Say?* (Glasgow, 1982), but thereafter, contrary to Kelman and Leonard, his career saw little progress.
7. In the following the stories are quoted from the original edition, which has no page numbers. The stories were later reprinted, with minor alterations, in various collections.
8. Alasdair Gray, *Lanark* (Edinburgh, 1981), 491.
9. 'bit', clearly a misprint, was corrected as 'but' when the story was included in *The Burn* (London, 1991), 123.
10. *Scotsman*, 19 March 1983; *Times Educational Supplement*, 4 March 1983; *British Book News* (August 1983); *London Review of Books*, 5/7, 21 April–4 May 1983.
11. 'He knew him well' saw the light in *EMU Magazine* (1972), published by the Extramural Department of Glasgow University.
12. However, Puckerbrush Press, Orono, Maine, which holds the rights, brought out a second edition of the volume in 1992.
13. Postscript to *Lean Tales* (London, 1985), 287.

14. For Hobsbaum's own account see his essay, 'The Glasgow Group', *Edinburgh Review*, 80–1 (1988), 58–63.
15. Stuart Cosgrove and David Campbell, 'Behind the Wee Smiles', *New Statesman*, 16 December 1988.

CHAPTER 3. UNSETTLINGLY SETTLED

1. Duncan McLean, 'James Kelman Interviewed', *Edinburgh Review*, 71 (1985), 77–8.
2. Isobel Murray in *Scotsman*, 1 March 1984.
3. Cairns Craig, 'Resisting Arrest: James Kelman', in Gavin Wallace and Randall Stevenson (eds.), *The Scottish Novel since the Seventies* (Edinburgh, 1993), 109.
4. McLean, 'Kelman Interviewed', 69.
5. Kelman's idiosyncratic writing together of normally hyphenated or separate words extends in this novel to 'busdriver', 'newdriver', 'deskclerk' and 'lowerdeck'. His practice is not limited to a contraction of nouns, as in the German language, where you can freely do this. Kelman may have been influenced here by fellow-Glaswegian George Friel, whose pages are littered with similar contractions; see his novel *Mr Alfred M.A.* (1972).
6. Craig, 'Resisting Arrest', 105.
7. The song is by Alain Souchon.
8. To be sure, Kelman's obsession with numbers goes beyond the stakes, as his interest in mathematics and its relation to philosophy demonstrates. He variously refers to the mathematical logician Kurt Gödel or the Pythagoreans' preoccupations with figures. See his essay 'A Reading from Noam Chomsky and the Scottish Tradition in the Philosophy of Common Sense', in *'And the Judges Said . . .'*, 150, 182; and *A Disaffection*, 14, 36–7.
9. Craig, 'Resisting Arrest', 106–7.
10. Kirsty McNeill, 'Interview with James Kelman', *Chapman*, 57 (1989), 7.

CHAPTER 4. AUTHORITY FLOUTED

1. Kirsty McNeill, 'Interview with James Kelman', *Chapman*, 57 (1989), 5.
2. The use of this phrase, which is Glaswegian for 'go shopping', suggests that the entire trio is Scottish.
3. Blurb of *Hardie and Baird & Other Plays*.

4. The historical Andrew Hardie used that phrase when interrogated; see the entry on the rebel by Peter Holt in *Biographical Dictionary of Modern British Radicals*, vol. i, *1770–1830*, eds. Joseph O. Baylen and Norbert J. Gossman (Sussex, 1979), 205. There is also a good historical account of the Rising by Malcolm I. Thomis and Peter Holt in *Threats of Revolution in Britain 1789–1848* (London, 1977), 75–81, which rejects the view that an *agent provocateur* stirred the men into action. Kelman's play appears more coloured by P. Berresford Ellis and S. Mac A'Ghobhainn, *The Scottish Insurrection of 1820* (London, 1970). In his essay 'Prisons' Kelman refers to the research gone into the play, *Some Recent Attacks*, 55.

5. Shortly before his execution, Baird was actually visited by several members of his family; cf. Peter Holt, 'Baird, John', in *Biographical Dictionary of Modern British Radicals*, i., 25.

6. Hardie's account of the Rising was published as a pamphlet, *The Radical Revolt* (Rutherglen, n.d.).

7. Gerard Carruthers, one of the few critics to have seen the production of *One, Two – Hey!*, characterizes it as follows: 'The juxtaposition of the band's lively arrangements of classic rock songs with Kelman's well-observed drawing of the precarious and often boring mechanics of running a gigging band on a shoestring makes for an emotional see-sawing for the audience' ('James Kelman', *Post-war Literatures in English*, 35 [1997], 11). The story version of *The Art of the Big Bass Drum* is 'Comic Cuts' in *The Good Times*.

8. More about this affair and Kelman's subsequent prolonged correspondence with the Scottish Arts Council is in William Clark, 'A Conversation with James Kelman', *Variant*, 2/12 (2001), 3–7.

9. Tom Leonard's untitled poem opens with the lines 'And their judges spoke with one dialect / but the condemned spoke with many voices', *Situations Theoretical and Contemporary* (Newcastle, 1986), no page numbers.

10. E. J. Hobsbawm, *Bandits* (Harmondsworth, 1972), 51.

11. The autobiographical chapters include the title essay 'Elitism and English Literature, Speaking as a Writer', 'Say Hello to John La Rose' and 'When I Was That Age Did Art Exist?', a talk to schoolchildren in Texas; also some bits and pieces from the Introduction.

12. Raymond Chandler, 'Notes (Very Brief, Please) on English and American Style', *The Notebooks of Raymond Chandler and English Summer*, ed. Frank MacShane (London, 1976), 20, 22.

13. In the interview with Duncan McLean, Kelman concedes that point ('James Kelman Interviewed', *Edinburgh Review*, 71 (1985), 66–7.

14. The only critical article to explore this connection is Uwe Zagratzki's '"Blues fell this morning": James Kelman's Scottish Literature and Afro-American Music', *Scottish Literary Journal*, 27/1 (2000), 105–17.
15. The review appeared in *Glasgow Herald*, October 1985 (the exact date on the newspaper cutting furnished by Marion Sinclair of Polygon is illegible). Dunn reiterated his views in 'Divergent Scottishness: William Boyd, Alan Massie, Ronald Frame' in Gavin Wallace and Randall Stevenson (eds.), *The Scottish Novel since the Seventies*, (Edinburgh, 1993) 149–50. But see also David Hall, 'The Herald Essay: The Duty of a Novelist', *Glasgow Herald*, 16 September 1995.

CHAPTER 5. CONTACTS, TENSIONS, EMOTIONS

1. When contrasted with the story 'Street-sweeper' in *The Burn*, the irony is that in a similar situation somebody gets sacked for having neglected his duty owing to his giving first aid to a prone man. The absurd argument of the gaffer is: 'Your job's taking care of the streets, he's on the fucking pavement' (p. 81).
2. Douglas Gifford, 'Discovering Lost Voices', *Books in Scotland*, 38 (1991), 4.
3. Ian A. Bell, 'James Kelman', *New Welsh Review*, 10 (1990) 20–1; Stephen Bernstein, 'James Kelman', *Review of Contemporary Fiction*, 20/3 (2000), 59–60.
4. 'the Hon' (now with the article in the lower case) and 'Sarah Crosbie' are reprinted from *Short Tales from the Night Shift*.
5. J. D. Macarthur believes there are even two external third-person narrators in the story; see his 'The Narrative Voice in James Kelman's *The Burn*', *Studies in English Literature* (Tokyo), English number, 71 (1995), 191.
6. Bernstein, 'James Kelman', 63.
7. Francis Spufford, review of *Greyhound for Breakfast*, *London Review of Books*, 9/7, 2 April 1987.

CHAPTER 6. UNDER SURVEILLANCE, RESISTING

1. Louis Althusser, 'Ideology and Ideological State Apparatuses', in his *Lenin and Philosophy and Other Essays* (London, 1971), 155.
2. 'Von hier und heute geht eine neue Epoche der Weltgeschichte aus, und ihr könnt sagen, ihr seid dabei gewesen' ('Here and now begins a new era in the world's history, and you can say that you were present at its birth' – my translation, HGK), quoted in Wilhelm

Bode, *Goethes Leben*, continued by Valerian Tornius, *1790–1794: Vereinsamung* (Berlin, 1926), 161.

3. Johann Wolfgang von Goethe, *Die Leiden des jungen Werthers*, book One, 12 August.

4. The reference to the French title of Michel Foucault's *Discipline and Punish* (English translation 1977) does, as in the case of Althusser's 'Ideology and Ideological State Apparatuses' essay, not necessarily imply that Kelman has read these works – neither Foucault nor Althusser are directly referred to in the essay volume *'And the Judges Said . . .'* – but he was certainly familiar with the ideas expressed in them.

5. Ian A. Bell, 'Form and Ideology in Contemporary Scottish Fiction', in Susanne Hagemann (ed.), *Studies in Scottish Fiction: 1945 to the Present* (Frankfurt, 1996), 231.

6. Cf. also 'Old Holborn' from the same collection and the expanded dramatized version of it, *The Busker*, discussed in Chapter 4.

7. Craig's title 'Resisting Arrest' has, of course, more than one meaning. It also alludes to Kelman's restless characters (resisting 'a rest') and the initially unattractive idiom of much of the fiction.

8. Drew Milne points to the ironic use of this and other terms in the novel: 'terrortory', perhaps a false pronunciation, invites a reading of 'terror Tory'. See his article 'Broken English: James Kelman's *Translated Accounts*', *Edinburgh Review*, 108 (2002), 106–15.

9. Kirsty McNeill, 'Interview with James Kelman', *Chapman*, 57 (1989), 6.

10. Keith Miller, *Times Literary Supplement*, 8 June 2001.

Bibliography

WORKS BY JAMES KELMAN (BRITISH FIRST EDITIONS AND CURRENT PAPERBACKS LISTED ONLY)

Three Glasgow Writers (with Alex. Hamilton and Tom Leonard) (Glasgow: Molendinar Press, 1976).

Short Tales from the Night Shift (Glasgow: Print Studio Press, 1978).

Not Not While the Giro and Other Stories (Edinburgh: Polygon, 1983; London: Vintage, 1989).

The Busconductor Hines (Edinburgh: Polygon, 1984).

A Chancer (Edinburgh: Polygon, 1985; London: Vintage, 1995).

Lean Tales (with Alasdair Gray and Agnes Owens) (London: Cape, 1985).

Greyhound for Breakfast (London: Secker & Warburg, 1987; London: Vintage, 1996). Short stories.

A Disaffection (London: Secker & Warburg, 1989; London: Vintage, 1999).

The Burn (London: Secker & Warburg, 1991; London: Vintage, 1992). Short stories.

Hardie and Baird & Other Plays (London: Secker & Warburg, 1991).

Some Recent Attacks: Essays Cultural & Political (Stirling: AK Press, 1992).

How Late it Was, How Late (London: Secker & Warburg, 1994; London: Vintage, 1995).

The Good Times (London: Secker & Warburg, 1998). Short stories.

Translated Accounts (London: Secker & Warburg, 2001; London: Vintage, 2002).

'And the Judges Said . . .': Essays (London: Secker & Warburg, 2002; London: Vintage, 2003).

You Have to be Careful in the Land of the Free (London: Hamish Hamilton, 2004).

LONGER PRINT INTERVIEWS

Clark, William, 'A Conversation with James Kelman', *Variant*, 2/12 (2001), 3–7. A Kelman very upset by the refusal of Scottish theatres to produce his new play and, more generally, by the bloody-mindedness of Scottish cultural administrators.

McLean, Duncan, 'James Kelman Interviewed', *Edinburgh Review*, 71 (1985), 64–80. Essential reading for the early Kelman. deals in depth with class assumptions about literature, contemporary English novelists, the use of 'swear words' (a term rejected by the author) and narrative technique in *The Busconductor Hines* and *A Chancer*.

McNeill, Kirsty, 'Interview with James Kelman', *Chapman*, 57 (1989), 1–9. On narrative voice and the elitist value system implicit in Standard English, on working-class intellectuals and the figures of Hines, Tammas and Doyle.

Ross, Raymond, 'Travels from Maryhill to the "mainstream" and back', *Scotsman*, 12 February 1983. A source of biographical information about Kelman's early life, the 'literary company' he kept and valued, and the existentialist dilemma of being 'free to commit suicide, but not as long as the social security cheque comes in', the double negation of 'Not not while the giro'.

Vericat, Fabio, 'An Interview with James Kelman', *Barcelona Review*, 28 (January–February 2002) [on-line review]. Short answers to questions about emigration from Scotland as a solution for the characters in the novels, Scottish and Spanish football teams and the themes of *Translated Accounts*.

AUDIO CASSETTE

Seven Stories, read by the author, Sound House-AK Productions (1997–8).

CRITICAL STUDIES

Baker, Simon, '"Wee stories with a working-class theme": The Reimagining of Urban Realism in the Fiction of James Kelman', in Susanne Hagemann (ed.), *Studies in Scottish Fiction: 1945 to the Present* (Frankfurt, 1996), 235–50. Compares the author's treatment of urban experience favourably with less successful attempts by

Welsh writers to come to terms with it.
Bell, Ian A., 'James Kelman', *New Welsh Review*, 10 (1990), 18–22. A brief,
    but immensely suggestive review of the fiction up to *A Disaffection*.
    Situates Kelman in the national cultural and political context of
    Scotland.
Bernstein, Stephen, 'James Kelman', *Review of Contemporary Fiction*, 20/3
    (2000), 42–80. A fastidious work-by-work overview of Kelman's
    career from his beginnings to *The Good Times*, complete with a
    Kelman checklist and glimpses of American responses to the œuvre.
Bittenbender, J. C., 'Silence, Censorship, and the Voices of *Skaz* in the
    Fiction of James Kelman', *Bucknell Review*, 43/2 (2000), 150–65. A
    reading of Kelman in the light of Mikhail Bakhtin's writings about
    language, dialogue and double-voiced discourse. Problematic in its
    frequent collapsing of narrative and character voice.
Böhnke, Dietmar, *Kelman Writes Back: Literary Politics in the Work of a
    Scottish Writer* (Berlin, 1999). Wide coverage of topics, though little
    specific analysis of individual works.
Burgess, Moira, *Imagine a City: Glasgow in Fiction* (Glendaruel, 1998),
    passim. Brief informed discussions of the major stages in Kelman's
    career by the historian of the Glasgow novel. Alert to his 'totally
    distinctive, sensitive and accurate, yet variable style'.
Carruthers, Gerald, 'James Kelman', *Post-War Literatures in English*, 35
    (1997), 1–12. A comprehensive précis of the entire œuvre up to *How
    Late it Was, How Late*.
Craig, Cairns, 'Resisting Arrest: James Kelman', in Gavin Wallace and
    Randall Stevenson (eds)., *The Scottish Novel since the Seventies*
    (Edinburgh, 1993), 99–114. The most sustained discussion of the
    novels and their philosophical foundation, existentialism, up to *A
    Disaffection*.
Daly, Macdonald, 'Your Average Working Kelman', in his *Crackpot Texts*
    (London, 1997), 17–24. A harsh critique, written in mock Glaswe-
    gian, of Kelman's voice and putative philosophical confusions,
    especially in the novel here dubbed 'A Disaffectant'.
Dixon, Keith, 'Punters and Smoky Breath: The Writing of James
    Kelman', *Écosse: Littérature et Civilisation*, 9 (1990), 65–77. A
    discussion of *The Busconductor Hines* and *A Chancer* centring on
    the title figures' lives on the edge.
Edinburgh Review, 108 (2002). A special section on 'Kelman and
    Commitment' edited by Ellen-Raïssa Jackson and Willy Maley:
    seven essays on Kelman and masculinity, the commitment to place,
    The Busconductor Hines, A Chancer, Some Recent Attacks and *Translated
    Accounts* (details under contributors' names).
Engledow, Sarah, 'Studying Form: The Off-the-Page Politics of *A
    Chancer*', *Edinburgh Review*, 108 (2002), 69–84. Challenging existential

readings of the novel, this original sociologically informed study emphasizes the anarchic economics of gambling and views Tammas's actions as instances of an 'off-the page' politics of Kelman's work.

Freeman, Alan, 'The Humanist's Dilemma: A Polemic against Kelman's Polemics', *Edinburgh Review*, 108 (2002), 28–40. Critical of Kelman the essayist's sweeping generalizations in his discussions of censorship, the role of artists and the slate; sees these views conflicting with the individual and local detail fleshed out in the fiction.

Gifford, Douglas, 'Discovering Lost Voices', *Books in Scotland*, 38 (1991), 1–6. A penetrating review of Kelman's progress as a short-story writer and a brief discussion of the plays.

—— 'James Kelman (b. 1946)', in Douglas Gifford et al. (eds.), *Scottish Literature in English and Scots* (Edinburgh, 2002), 872–83. A collage of the author's reviews in *Books in Scotland*.

Gilbert, Geoff, 'Can Fiction Swear? James Kelman and the Booker Prize', in Rod Mengham (ed.), *An Introduction to Contemporary Fiction* (Cambridge, 1999), 219-34. Draws on J. L. Austin's 'speech-act theory' to discuss the various functions of the curse in Kelman's fiction, and to explain the hostile media reception of *How Late it Was, How Late*.

Kirk, John, 'Figuring the Dispossessed: Images of the Urban Working Class in the Writing of James Kelman', *English*, 48/191 (1999), 101–16. Interesting discussions of the representation of city life in some stories from *Greyhound for Breakfast* and *The Burn*, as well as the union meeting in *The Busconductor Hines*, but marred by inaccurate quotations and references.

Klaus, H. Gustav, 'James Kelman: A Voice from the Lower Depths of Thatcherite Britain', *London Magazine*, 29/5–6 (1989), 39–48. Relates the emergence of Kelman's angry voice to the social and political climate under Thatcherism.

—— 'Kelman for Beginners', *Journal of the Short Story in English*, 22 (1994), 127–35. Proposes the short stories as the best entry into Kelman's world. Introduces the term 'speaker-narrator' for Kelman's characters.

—— 1984 Glasgow: Alasdair Gray, Tom Leonard, James Kelman', *Etudes écossaises*, 2 (1993), 31–40. Discusses aspects of class, work and language in three works from that year; the Kelman section is devoted to *The Busconductor Hines*.

Knights, Ben, ' "The Wean and That": Paternity and Domesticity in *The Busconductor Hines*', in his *Writing Masculinities* (Basingstoke, 1999), 180–94. Points to the vulnerability of Kelman's males and to the language of wit, subversion and cunning as the terrain on which masculine identities emerge.

Macarthur, J. D, 'The Narrative Voice in James Kelman's *The Burn*', *Studies in English Literature* [Tokyo], English number, 71 (1995), 181–95. Distinguishes between 'monologue', 'interior monologue' and 'third-person narrative', though the first term does not quite catch what he is after.

MacDonald, Graeme, 'A Scottish Subject? Kelman's Determination', *Études écossaises*, 8 (2002), 89–111. An informed, if not jargon-free discussion of the elusive Scottishness of Kelman's work based on snippets from the later fiction.

————, 'Dépasser ces putains de limites: Zola, Kelman et les voix ouvrières', in David Kinloch and Richard Price (eds.), *La Nouvelle Alliance: Influences francophones sur la littérature écossaise moderne* (Grenoble, 2000), 147–76. Traces a number of instructive parallels between the writing projects of the two authors, and also the hostile responses to their agenda.

McGlynn, Mary, '"Middle-Class Wankers" and Working-Class Texts: The Critics and James Kelman', *Contemporary Literature*, 43/1 (2002), 50–84. Studded with glib phrases and wilful references to other writers, this wordy discussion of *How Late* and *A Disaffection* does a disservice to the study of working-class writing it purports to defend.

McMillan, Neil, 'Wilting or the "Poor Wee Boy Syndrome": Kelman and Masculinity', *Edinburgh Review*, 108 (2002), 41–55. Sees Kelman, while sensitive to the representation of gender, as shying away from a more positive engagement with the transformed role of masculinity; exemplified in a discussion of *The Busconductor Hines*.

McMunnigall, Allan, and Carruthers, Gerard, 'Locating Kelman: Glasgow, Scotland and the Commitment to Place', *Edinburgh Review*, 108 (2002), 56–68. Looks at Kelman's place in the history of Scottish writing and points to the differences between his generally sober dispossessed lives and the crassly violent and hedonistic lives in the fiction of Irvine Welsh, Duncan McLean and Alan Warner, for which Kelman created a space.

Maley, Willy, 'Swearing Blind: Kelman and the Curse of the Working Classes', *Edinburgh Review*, 95 (1996), 105–12. Focuses on the public controversy over the many 'fucks' in *How Late it Was, How Late* in order to defend Kelman's considered use of 'swearing'.

Miller, Karl, 'Glasgow Hamlet', in his *Authors* (Oxford, 1989), 156–62. Portrays the protagonist of *A Disaffection* and his interior monologues in these terms.

Milne, Drew, 'James Kelman: Dialectics of Urbanity', in James A. Davies et al. (eds.), *Writing Region and Nation* (Swansea, 1994), 393–407. Focuses on Kelman's attempt to represent factual reality through a narrative voice that does not impose itself on character. Finds this more successfully realized in the short fiction.

———— 'Broken English: James Kelman's *Translated Accounts*', *Edinburgh Review*, 108 (2002), 106–15. Sees the novel shot through with indeterminacy and irony, and consequently politically more ambiguous than its predecessors.

Nicoll, Laurence, ' "This is not a nationalist position": James Kelman's Existential Voice', *Edinburgh Review*, 103 (2000), 79–84. A pithy exposition of the author's existentialist stance, and how it informs his writing in terms of locality and contingency.

———— 'Gogol's Overcoat: Kelman *Resartus*', *Edinburgh Review*, 108 (2002), 116–22. Following a hint by Kelman, the essay discusses what the author may have learnt in terms of narrative structure and open-endedness from nineteenth-century Russian novelists.

Pitchford, Nicola, 'How Late it was for England: James Kelman's Scottish Booker Prize', *Contemporary Literature*, 41/4 (2000), 693–725. Examines the cultural significance of the annual Booker Prize ritual and registers a strange collusion between Kelman's conservative detractors in England and upholders of traditional notions of Scottish culture.

Prillinger, Horst, *Family and the Scottish Working-Class Novel 1984–1994* (Frankfurt, 2000), *passim*. Notes the absence of community in Kelman's novels and the disintegration not only of family life, but also of the central individual.

Sellin, Bernard, 'James Kelman, *The Busconductor Hines* et la réalité ouvrière', *Études écossaises*, 3 (1996), 129–40. Perceptive discussion of the reified universe confronting Hines and of his growing sense of alienation.

Spinks, Lee, 'In Juxtaposition to Which: Narrative, System and Subjectivity in the Fiction of James Kelman', *Edinburgh Review*, 108 (2002), 85–105. As the title announces, a long theoretical exposition, followed by a no less vertiginously abstract discussion of *A Disaffection.*

Vice, Sue, 'Dialogism and Reported Speech in James Kelman, *How Late it Was, How Late*', in her *Introducing Bakhtin* (Manchester, 1997), 91–102. Analyzes the mixing of direct with indirect and free indirect discourse in the novel, with the attendant pronominal shift from 'I' to 'ye' and 'he'.

Zagratzki, Uwe, ' "Blues fell this morning": James Kelman's Scottish Literature and Afro-American Music', *Scottish Literary Journal*, 27/1 (2000), 105–17. Sees a parallel between black oral culture as articulated in blues songs and the voices as well as precarious positions of Kelman's struggling characters.

Index

Recent and Forthcoming Titles in the New Series of

WRITERS AND THEIR WORK

WRITERS AND THEIR WORK

RECENT & FORTHCOMING TITLES

RECENT & FORTHCOMING TITLES

RECENT & FORTHCOMING TITLES

TITLES IN PREPARATION

Title	Author
Fleur Adcock	*Janet Wilson*
Ama Ata Aidoo	*Nana Wilson-Tagoe*
Matthew Arnold	*Kate Campbell*
Margaret Atwood	*Marion Wynne-Davies*
John Banville	*Peter Dempsey*
William Barnes	*Christopher Ricks*
Black British Writers	*Deidre Osborne*
William Blake	*Steven Vine*
Charlotte Brontë	*Stevie Davies*
Robert Browning	*John Woodford*
Basil Bunting	*Martin Stannard*
John Bunyan	*Tamsin Spargoe*
Children's Writers of the 19th Century	*Mary Sebag-Montefiore*
Coriolanus	*Anita Pacheco*
Cymbeline	*Peter Swaab*
Douglas Dunn	*David Kennedy*
David Edgar	*Peter Boxall*
T. S. Eliot	*Colin MacCabe*
J. G. Farrell	*John McLeod*
Nadine Gordimer	*Lewis Nkosi*
Geoffrey Grigson	*R. M. Healey*
David Hare	*Jeremy Ridgman*
Ted Hughes	*Susan Bassnett*
The Imagist Poets	*Andrew Thacker*
Ben Jonson	*Anthony Johnson*
A. L. Kennedy	*Dorothy McMillan*
Jack Kerouac	*Michael Hrebebiak*
Jamaica Kincaid	*Susheila Nasta*
Rudyard Kipling	*Jan Montefiore*
Rosamond Lehmann	*Judy Simon*
Una Marson & Louise Bennett	*Alison Donnell*
Norman MacCaig	*Alasdair Macrae*
Thomas Middleton	*Hutchings & Bromham*
John Milton	*Nigel Smith*
Much Ado About Nothing	*John Wilders*
R. K. Narayan	*Shirley Chew*
New Woman Writers	*Marion Shaw/Lyssa Randolph*
Ngugi wa Thiong'o	*Brendon Nicholls*
Religious Poets of the 17th Century	*Helen Wilcox*
Samuel Richardson	*David Deeming*
Olive Schreiner	*Carolyn Burdett*
Sam Selvon	*Ramchand & Salick*
Olive Senior	*Denise de Canes Narain*
Mary Shelley	*Catherine Sharrock*
Charlotte Smith & Helen Williams	*Angela Keane*
Ian Crichton Smith	*Colin Nicholson*
R. L. Stevenson	*David Robb*
Tom Stoppard	*Nicholas Cadden*
Elizabeth Taylor	*N. R. Reeve*
Dylan Thomas	*Chris Wiggington*
Three Avant-Garde Poets	*Peter Middleton*
Three Lyric Poets	*William Rowe*

TITLES IN PREPARATION

Title	Author
Derek Walcott	*Stephen Regan*
Jeanette Winterson	*Gina Vitello*
Women's Poetry at the Fin de Siècle	*Anna Vadillo*
William Wordsworth	*Nicola Trott*